Zerubbabel Leadership:
Rebuilding the Temple

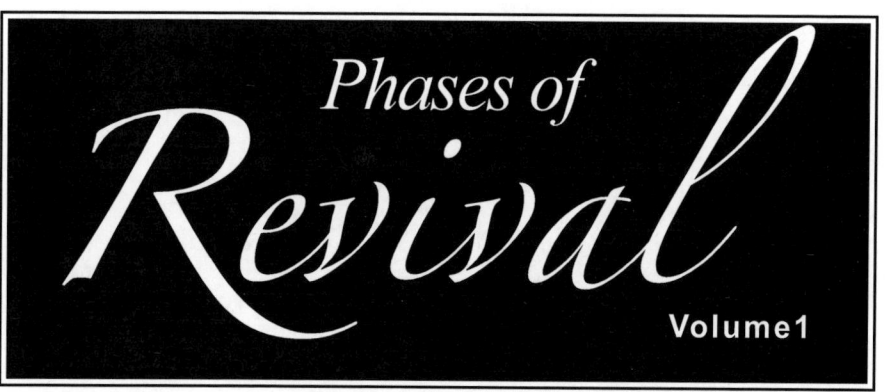

K. BOBIE AMANKWATIA

Copyright © 2011 by K. Bobie Amankwatia

All rights reserved. No part of this book may be used, reproduced, stored in a retrieval system, or transmitted in any form whatsoever — including electronic, photocopy, recording — without prior written permission from the author, except in the case of brief quotations embodied in critical articles or reviews.

All scripture quotations, unless otherwise indicated, are taken from the *Holy Bible, The New King James Study Bible*. Thomas Nelson.

FIRST EDITION

ISBN: 9780982947654

Library of Congress Control Number: 2011921629

Published by
NewBookPublishing.com, a division of Reliance Media, Inc.
2395 Apopka Blvd., #200, Apopka, FL 32703
NewBookPublishing.com

Printed in the United States of America

Table of Contents

Dedication 5

Preface 7

Acknowledgements 11

1. The Need For Revival 13
2. Leaving Your Comfort Zone 25
3. Prayer: The Right Priority Of Revival Leadership 39
4. Putting Faith Into Action 49
5. Laying A Sound Foundation In Revival Times 57
6. Readiness To Battle The Enemy 81
7. The Waiting Period 97
8. The Anointing Oil 113
9. Steps To Receiving A Flesh Anointing/Renewal 135

About The Author 149

Dedication

To my beautiful, loving and gracious wife Tonya and my precious and wonderful sons, Scott and Daniel, whose prayers, love and encouragement kept me focused to complete this volume.

This book is also dedicated to the loving memory of my gracious father and my only role model, J. B. Amankwatia, who went home to be with the Lord in 1995, and to my sweet and loving mother Dora, who has never ceased to lift my family up before the Lord daily. Their loving and gracious parental guidance helped prepare me to become the godly husband and father I am today. I am forever grateful to them.

To my younger brother King Opoku Amankwatia, whose love and friendship from our childhood has meant a great deal to me. Also dedicated to my darling niece, Josephine Amankwatia, whose graciousness has given my mother a great joy.

A very special dedication goes to my spiritual mother and prayer partner, Jayne Humburger and her lovely and caring daughter, "Lady" Becky, whose love, support and encouragement challenged me not to give up on this project.

Also dedicated to my best friend Bob Metrision and his darling wife Bonnie.

A special dedication to the memory of the late Norman Haupt, a dedicated elder and a wonderful Sunday School teacher, Rev David G Kai, a pioneering servant of the Lord and Isaac Kumi, a giant of the faith. May they rest joyfully in the arms of the loving Savior.

Preface

Phases of Revival has come about after years of pastoring, teaching, planting churches and counseling. During these many years of ministry, I have observed some serious problems within the church which are so often overlooked, especially when a church is growing in monetary worth and membership. Unfortunately, in most circles, both types of growth have become the measure of spiritual growth or revival. As a result, many of those in leadership have been blinded to their own spiritual needs and that of their congregations.

Some leaders have even come to see a change in the style of worship as a sign of revival or renewal. In the absence of genuine spiritual renewal, the styles of music are nothing more than a way to stir up emotional excitement among the congregation. Thus, many people leave the emotionalism of the services only to find themselves in the same spiritually deficient state. Leaders who are sensitive to these spiritual deficiencies often find themselves frustrated and discouraged because they can hardly move the congregation beyond the status quo.

I have also noted the cultural and governmental policies in our world and their impact on the Bible believing church. These make it an urgent obligation of the church to move forward with faith and boldness to change the world with a demonstration of the power of the gospel of Jesus Christ. Only the gospel of Christ can change the world and bring about a healthy level of sanity. But the lukewarm attitude of the church makes this impossible. As a result, the cries for renewal have never been louder at any time in human history than they are now.

The *Phases of Revival* affords believers an opportunity to examine some sound biblical principles to revival leadership. It covers the ministry priority of revival leadership that will bring about renewal among church leaders and their congregations. Zerubbabel leadership principles in leading the Israelites from their Babylonian bondage and turning desolation into vibrancy and active worship, turning delays in ministry into moments of waiting on the Lord to renew our strength are also discussed in the book to encourage the church to stay focused in spite of hindrances along the way.

The following subjects are covered in this volume:
- Prayer as leadership priority
- Putting faith into action

- The waiting period in revival times
- Readiness for battle in the midst of revival
- The anointing oil
- Steps to receiving a flesh anointing/renewal

These subjects, as they are addressed in this volume, enable the reader to identify and apply the Zerubbabel principles in their lives and their ministries to achieve effective leadership outcomes.

Acknowledgements

I would like to thank many people dear to my heart whose love, prayerful support and challenge stirred up a level of motivation within me to prepare *Phases of Revival: Zerubbabel Leadership - Rebuilding the Temple*. My deepest appreciation and gratitude go to Mark and Pam Jones, who assimilated my family and me into their lovely family and made our relocation to Pennsylvania a joyful and blessed event.

A special acknowledgement to our precious friends Bill and Donna DiSciacca, who have always been there for us. My gratitude also goes to my "twin brother" Jim Moore and his lovely wife Julie for all the quality time spent with them that stirred up some spiritual insights towards this project. I am also grateful to Mike and Tammy Kissel for their great testimonies of the power of prayer. My sincere appreciation and gratitude to Jim Brashear, pastor of Bethany UMC, whose ministry has greatly blessed my family and me. My loving gratitude also goes to Glenn Han, a gentle spirited worship leader and "my little brother" Phil G. Thomas. My gratitude also to Drs. Avril Livingstone and J. A. Williams who helped steered my spiritual and theological persuasion, and to Alex A. Waklatsi , a great brother in Christ and "mentor". The moral and spiritual contributions to my life by my sweet, lovely and beautiful sisters, Florence Kwakwa, Dinah Osei-Boateng and my patient and caring brother, Robert Kyei Yamoah cannot be over looked. It is always a sweet communion when in their presence.

A great gratitude from me and my family to Asamoah G Amankwatia, Senior Pastor and all the leaders and members of the Royal Gate Mission Church of Ghana, West Africa, for their prayers and all the kind words of encouragement.

To God be all the glory, for putting such wonderful and precious people in my life.

Chapter One

The Need For Revival

Every revival or spiritual awakening in the church of Jesus Christ can be orchestrated only by God. No human can invent or initiate spiritual revivals; they are the expressed work of the Holy Spirit. Throughout history, revival has often been preceded by a period of "darkness" in which righteousness gave way to unrighteousness and religious rituals that did not enhance Christian maturity. Dark periods replaced truth with deceitfulness and substituted holiness with a "new morality" of sensuality that many embraced.

The Church

In dark times, God is not just denied but is also forgotten. Even within the Christian community, God is hardly mentioned during the week. Most reduce God to viral email forwards in their daily lives, while some keep him on their Sunday morning To-Do list, but only for one and a half hours. In an effort to generate a spiritual revival, the church has often turned to multiple programs and activities chosen to create a level of emotional excitement. But these human efforts exclude the Holy Spirit and can never substitute for true spiritual awakening.

In fact, such programs only contribute to the adulteration of holy, God-filled worship. For example, in many church circles the dominant message becomes "I decree" and "I declare" statements and pseudo blessings, stirring up emotions at the expense of sound biblical teachings. Congregants rarely hear message of the cross, an omission which is devastating. The gospel's strength and demonstration of power in the early church were rooted in the preaching of the cross. Still, some denominations today have even gone to great lengths to remove all references to the "blood" of Jesus from their hymn books. Could it be that the church is trying to be politically correct? After all, God entrusted the church with the message of the cross of *offense* **(see Galatians, 5 and 6).**

Moreover, integrity seems to be disappearing from church teachings. Many preachers are bent on using their congregations to build up their personal ministries instead of using their ministries to build up their congregations. Many churches today are being managed by CEOs rather than men and women who are called of God and filled with His Spirit. A number of contemporary preachers have largely turned to motivational speaking rather than proclaiming the uncompromising truth of the gospel, which is the power of God unto salvation **(see Romans, 1:17).**

We seem to be heading towards a dark age of unprecedented apostasy. Some denominations welcome deviant sexual behaviors which are condemned by scripture **(see Romans, 1:26-38)** as an acceptable lifestyle, even for its ministers and church leadership. Divorce rate within the church is surpassing that of the secular society. The era of Eli and his sons defiling [defying] the holy things of the Lord appears to be with us today **(see I Samuel, 1 – 4).** However, we should not lose heart, because there are many Hannahs on the fringes interceding to bring forth modern Samuels, men and women willing to fill the pulpits and declare the oracles of the living God.

The Culture

Homes, communities and nations have been saturated with various societal icons of immorality. Promiscuity and sexual perversion pepper education, industry, popular media and worldwide entertainment. Cultural relativism is dominating our society. The societal values and norms that formed the bedrock of our moral absolutes have given way to the concept of "everything goes." The increasing reality is that the "spirit" of Sodom and Gomorrah is with us today. The Bible and prayer have been thrown out of our public schools. Even, institutions of higher learning, like Harvard, Yale and Princeton Universities which were established by Christian Leaders to train men and women in ministry and godly leadership have in modern times become some of the strongest opponents of the church and the gospel of Jesus Christ. The wrath of God is inevitable, unless there is a spiritual awakening to stir up the hearts of men and women to turn to Jesus Christ, the Savior of the world.

Governments

The governments of our world have turned the very institutions that should bring some sense of sanity to the nations into instruments that promote unrighteousness. Law after law is being promulgated to enhance the rapid decline of Judeo-Christian moral values. Lawmakers no longer hold themselves to high moral standards, and their way of thinking has trickled down to the masses. In this kind of environment, sin is almost revered while purity and righteousness have become objects of mockery. Political correctness has literally swept over the nations and the governments of our world. Public expression of one's faith in Jesus is mocked and totally shunned in the political arena. It has even been reported that the European Union's calendar for the year 2011 has the Jewish and Islamic holidays listed but all the Christian holidays which used to be on previous calendars have been removed. It is evident that the governments of the world are wholeheartedly receptive to everything except Christianity.

More and more, laws are completely anti-Christian. For example, legislation exists in Canada today making it unlawful for a minister to preach against homosexuality on the airways. A British hotel owner in Liverpool was taken to court for standing up for his faith against a Muslim. In the United States, some state governments and the federal government are pushing for laws that will legalize same-sex marriage. U.S. Hate Crime laws appear to target the church in an attempt to silence preaching against homosexuality. God's divine order is under attack from the rulers of this world. The Psalmist put it this way, **"The kings of the earth set themselves, and the rulers take counsel together, against the Lord, and against his Anointed" (Psalms 2:2).**

The Heavens Declare God's Anger

The spiritual and moral decline in the church and the culture only invite the judgment of God. Even the heavens, which are to declare God's glory, are under today's circumstances declaring divine wrath upon the earth in devastating proportions. The divine wrath from the heavens may be placed under these categories:

A) **The Heavens Are Shut:**

The Scriptures declare God's judgment upon his people for turning away from his statutes and precepts. **"And then the Lord's wrath will be kindled against you, and he shuts up the heavens, that there be no rains, and that the land yields not her fruit…"** (Deuteronomy **11: 17).** This implies that rebellion against God blocks or hinders our blessings. As a result, we cease to be fruitful and experience rapid moral and spiritual decline.

B) **The Heaven Over Us Is Stayed:**

Because of disobedience and the neglect of His work, the Lord spoke through prophet Haggai saying, **"Therefore the heaven over you is stayed from dew, and the earth is stayed from her fruit" (Haggai 1:10).** The heavens are closed and the earth is unfruitful because of man's rejection of divine order and choosing to do things his own way.

C) **The Heavens Are As Iron:**

"And I will break the pride of thy power, and I will make the heavens as iron and the earth as brass" (Leviticus 26:19&20). When we as a people become disobedient to the Lord, and reject His law, we incur His displeasure. Subsequently, we do not experience His glory, blessings and manifestation. It seems as if "ICHABAD" (*the glory has departed*) is written all over the nations of the earth.

D) **The Heavens And The Earth Aligned Against Mankind:**

When immorality took over the land and the people totally rejected Noah's warnings, both the heavens and the earth opened up with rain gushing from the skies and water from the ground to destroy both man and beast, except Noah's family and the pairs of animals and birds that were in the Ark with him. The Scripture declares, **"...the same day were all the fountains of the great deep broken up, and the windows of heaven opened" (Genesis 7:11).** Because of sin, nature had turned against mankind. That which should bless the earth and cause it to flourish turned into an instrument of wrath to bring destruction upon man and beast alike, because of man's wickedness.

In relating the curses that could befall them should they reject the statutes of the Lord, Moses said to the children of Israel, **"Moreover all these curses shall come upon thee, and shall pursue thee, and overtake thee, till thou be destroyed; because thou hearkened not unto the voice of the Lord thy God, to keep his commandments and his statutes which he commanded thee" (Deuteronomy 28:45).** When the Word of the Lord is rejected, it does lead to curses upon curses falling upon us. All the reports in the news of wars, political upheavals and uncertainties in the world do indeed suggest we must be under a curse.

Indeed, our world is experiencing a moral and spiritual heart failure. The blood vessels of our world are clogged with moral and spiritual cholesterol that needs to be removed before there is a massive heart attack. What the world truly needs more than anything to bring about healthy moral and spiritual resuscitation is not CPR, but "CCR," the Christ-Centered Renewal that can permeate the very core of our society and reach the depths of our spiritual depravity. This will necessitate a divine visitation.

God Still Wants To Visit His People

In spite of our numerous failures, God desires to visit us and bring down a mighty spiritual awakening that will turn many back to the cross. The following are just but a few of the Scriptures which do point to God's promise of visitation by the Holy Spirit.

"Blessed be the Lord God of Israel, for he hath visited and redeemed his people" (Luke 1:68).

"Thou hast granted me life and favor, and thy visitation hath preserved my spirit" (Job 10:12).

"Through the tender mercy of our God; whereby the dayspring from on high hath visited us" (Luke 1:78).

Because God wants to visit His people, He gave us basic spiritual principles on how best to approach His throne of grace and have the heavens opened for His outpouring and restoration. This spiritual principle is clearly laid out in **Isaiah 64:1,** saying **"Oh thou wouldest rend the heavens; that thou wouldest come down that the mountains might flow down at thy presence"** This passage affirms that people of God can pray and ask Him to "tear by force the heavens." This kind of prayer must be borne out of total surrender and willingness to walk in obedience to

His Lordship. This is a prayer of repentance, saying that we have recognized our failures and are ready to run into His opened and outstretched arms. The Lord clearly affirmed this in His response to Solomon's prayer saying,

"If I shut up the heavens that there be no rain, or if I command locust to devour the land or send pestilence on my people; if my people called by my name shall humble themselves, and pray, and seek my face, and turn from their wicked ways, then I will hear from heaven, and will forgive them their sins, and heal their land" (II Chronicles 13 &14).

In response to Solomon's prayer God gave a divine directive to rend or tear the heavens open for His people to experience an outpouring of His Spirit. If God's people will repent and turn back to Him like prodigal sons and daughters, He will receive us back unto Himself **(See Luke, 15:20-24).**

The Need For Revival Leadership

To bring about an awakening or revival, God has always chosen to partner with individuals irrespective of their race, color, creed, intellectual abilities, denominational background, social status or position in the church. God does though look for men and women who are both available and willing to pay the price so that they can lead His people in times of revival. These individuals are selfless, humble, and do not seek fame or glory for themselves. They are neither materialistic, nor prideful and do not use people to build their ministry, but rather use God's ministry to build up the people. They have one thing and one thing alone in mind: that the Lord would be glorified.

Ezekiel, the prophet, declared God's desire to partner with mankind to revive and restore His people in these words, **"And I sought for a man among them, that should make up the hedges, and stand in the gap before me for the land, that I should not destroy it; but I found none"** (Ezekiel 22:30). This was a sad day in the life of the nation. God's wishes met with a different response in the time of Prophet Isaiah, when the Lord called out, **"whom shall I send, and who will go for me?"** Isaiah replied, **"Here am I, send me"** (Isaiah 6:8).

David Livingstone responded to a similar call to Africa and paid the ultimate price; his life. It can be costly but we must understand that God's grace is always sufficient when we are obedient to the heavenly call. Apostle Paul came to this realization when the Lord said to him, **"My grace is sufficient for thee, for my strength is made perfect in weaknesses"** (II Corinthians 12:9).

Some of the men and women the Lord used to provide revival leadership to His people include Zerubbabel, Ezra, Nehemiah, David Livingstone, D.L. Moody, Billy Graham, Oral Roberts and Kathryn Kuhlman. And as in these individuals, there are specific qualities that the Lord requires in those He partners with in times of revival. The qualities or characteristics of such individuals include: humility **(Philippians 2:5-8)**, willingness to obey the voice of the Lord **(Acts 9:5-18)**, availability to be used by the Holy Spirit **(Isaiah 6:8)**, breaking away from customs and traditions so the Holy Spirit can use him/her to accomplish the will of the Father **(Acts 10:28-48)**, total dependence on the Lord **(II Chronicles 20:12)**, patience to wait on the Lord for wisdom and spiritual strength **(Isaiah 40:31)**, recognizing and accepting that all the glory belongs to the Lord and readiness to decrease that the Lord shall increase **(John 3:30).** Zerubbabel, by his leadership principles, demonstrated all these qualities which made him pliable and flexible in the hands of the Holy Spirit so that he could accomplish the Lord's purpose.

In this book we will discover Zerubbabel's response to God's call. We will learn the price Zerubbabel paid, the grace of God that was upon him, and his revival leadership principles. Zerubbabel's leadership principles included; leaving his comfort zone in obedience to the stirring of the Holy Spirit, prioritizing the building of the altar of God, responding to the prophetic insights which helped him lead the captives back to their ancestral home so that they could rebuild the temple and re-instituting the worship of the Living God in the face of fierce enemy attacks.

Chapter Two

Leaving Your Comfort Zone

"Who is among you of all his people? His God be with him, let him go up to Jerusalem, which is in Judah, and let him build the house of the Lord God of Israel, (he is the God,) which is in Jerusalem... Then rose the chief of the fathers of Judah and Benjamin, and the priest and the Levites with all them, whose spirit God had stirred, to go up to build the house of the Lord which is in Jerusalem." **(Ezra 1:3&5)**

The first major step for revival leadership is leaving our comfort zone to allow the Spirit of God to mold and shape us so that we may accomplish His purpose. Zerubbabel had to leave his home, his friends and the familiar customs and traditions. Church religious traditions, which are often rooted in denominational distinctive rather than in the Scripture, can be hindrances to spiritual awakening. Religiosity is different from a thoughtful, sincere adherence to Biblical truth. Religiosity is often rooted in humanistic ritualistic traditions which afford its adherents do's and don'ts rather than grace to serve the Lord. Such departure from religiosity is something that stems from the sovereign act of God in stirring our spirits to respond in total obedience to His perfect will.

The Spirit of God stirred the spirit of Zerubbabel and the elders to make the 700 mile-long journey back to Jerusalem. When God calls His people, He does not keep them where they are but rather moves them into a new dimension of spiritual release and purpose. Throughout Scripture and the history of the Church, God has stirred the spirit of men and women to leave their comfort zones and to move into total surrender to His sovereign will.

Leaving the comfort zone in order to move into God's will can produce miraculous outcomes. Such miraculous outcomes include: entering into divine inheritance, birthing a vision, the deliverance of the people of God, proclaiming Christ to the outcasts of society, and changing the world.

Entering Into Divine Inheritance

By leaving Babylon in obedience to the stirring of the Spirit of God, Zerubbabel was stepping out to retake possession of the Promised Land. The people of God had lost their inheritance and had been forced into bondage after neglecting the law of God. The enemy had taken control of their inheritance. This land was originally promised to Abraham when he left his ancestral home. The land of the Chaldeans was a familiar place of comfort but Abraham left it behind when his spirit was stirred by the Spirit of God. The Lord said to Abram (later called Abraham),

"Leave your country, your people and your father's household unto the land that I will show you. I will make you into a great nation and I will bless you. I will make your name great and you will be a blessing. I will bless those who bless you, and whosoever curses you, I will curse, and all peoples of the earth will be blessed through you" (Genesis 12:1-3). Zerubbabel knew of this promise and believed God to repossess it. He was willing to sacrifice everything in his life. He trusted the Lord to take back their inheritance. Nothing was going to stop him from moving forward.

His resolute faith and actions were like the lyrics of the song,

"Take the whole world and give me Jesus;
No turning back, no turning back:
The cross before me and the world behind me;
No turning back, no turning back."

This was also true with Ruth. This Moabitess left her country, her family and her father's house to follow Naomi to Bethlehem. Ruth's willingness to leave her comfort zone and follow with obedience eventually led to her marriage to Boaz and, by divine plan, inherited the blessings of sharing in the genealogy of Jesus Christ **(Ruth 1:15 – 16; Matthew 1:1-5).**

Zerubbabel left the place he had known all his life and returned to a place of desolation in order for God's word to be fulfilled **(see Isaiah, 44:28 and Jeremiah 25:12).** The first step toward possessing the inheritance is to leave our comfort zones of empty religion and man-made tradition in order to enter into an intimate relationship with the Almighty God. This requires that we not be entangled with the affairs of this life but rather keep our eyes on the one who has called us into His higher calling **(See II Timothy 2:4).** The church today is blessed with such abundance that some are caught up in maintaining our comfort instead of moving into His perfect will.

God has more to offer His people. Until Zerubbabel left Persia, he had no idea what great things the Lord could do with him and through him. The Lord made Zerubbabel a nation builder, a breach builder and a restorer of desolations. Our world now is broken, shattered and trampled by Satan and his hosts of demons. The church cannot continue at the same pace. It is time for the people of God to stand up and give a shout of faith with the words of the prophet Isaiah, "Here I am, send me."

Birthing A Vision

It is very important to note a resemblance in Zerubbabel's

ability to birth a vision after leaving his comfort zone and that of Jacob's ability to do the same. Jacob left Beersheba in obedience to Isaac, his father. That meant leaving the wells of Beersheba, which symbolized the family's wealth, and going into the depraved conditions of the hot desert roads of Padanaram. This obedience on Jacob's part brought him into a place of birthing a vision of the church.

The Bible tells us of Jacob falling asleep and having a vision of a ladder from the earth to the heavens and the Lord standing at the top of the ladder while angels ascended and descended. The Scripture says, **"And he lighted upon a certain place, and tarried there all night, because the sun was set, and he took of the stones of that place, and put there for his pillows, and laid down in that place to sleep" (Genesis 28:11).** The proper translation of the Hebrew text denotes a pregnant woman sitting on a birth stool to give birth. Jacob was indeed giving birth to the Church. He became the father of the patriarchs, the 12 tribes of Israel, from which Jesus the Messiah was born.

Our comfort zones, or our familiar grounds, can preoccupy our minds and blur our vision, and can keep us from recognizing what the Lord has in mind for us to accomplish. I believe this potential for preoccupation is one of the reasons leaders separate themselves from all distractions in the form of a spiritual retreat to seek the Lord. We have too much in our environment that distracts us from our spiritual pursuit of birthing a vision, and of hearing from God. Jacob experienced the Lord and named the place Bethel, which means "The House of God." Before being called Bethel the name of the place was Luz **(Genesis 28:19).**

Zerubbabel led the children of Israel into their inheritance where the vision of Jacob was to be fulfilled. The restored land was part of the preparation for the coming of the Messiah. Zerubbabel was able to give the people a vision of what the Lord had in store for them even though their circumstances dictated otherwise. By moving away from the distractions of Persia and moving into God's perfect will, Zerubbabel was able to develop the vision to move the people of God into higher heights in their spiritual worship.

Deliverance Of God's People

Revival leadership that requires leaving our comfort zone may usher us into situations that could mean life or death. When Zerubbabel left for Jerusalem, he did not know what to expect. He responded to God's call knowing quite well that **"there is nowhere God leads that He cannot provide grace for, and there is nothing God orders that He cannot pay for**." Zerubbabel found himself in some difficult times with challenges from all angles **(See Ezra 3:1&4).** Obedience to God's will does not mean everything is going to be a bouquet of roses. The enemy is bent on attacking us when we are doing God's will. We must keep in mind that the Lord will never leave us nor forsake us **(Matthew 28:20).**

When Moses was called by the Lord **"Come now therefore, and I will send thee unto Pharaoh, that thou mayest bring forth my people, the children of Israel out of Egypt" (Exodus 3:10)** he was afraid. Moses knew the potential consequences if Pharaoh should lay his hands on him. Moses had escaped from Pharaoh's wrath and was not prepared to go back and face him. He had made a family in the land of the Medians and had a safe life. He was outside the reach of Pharaoh. Moses was comfortable with his life as it was. However, the Lord called him to leave that place of comfort and to step into the arena of faith: becoming a great deliverer of Israel. When God's perfect time came for Moses to step forward into his pre-ordained leadership role, Moses initially balked. After obeying God and leaving the land of Midian, "Moses the coward and the fearful" became "Moses the courageous and the fearless" who delivered Israel from 400 years of slavery.

Often times, we turn our backs on the dying just because we do not want God to interfere with our comfortable lives. We must understand that the call to be witnesses in **Acts, 1:8** does not say stay in your comfort zone or your familiar territory, but rather to go even to the unknown territories. When we read the Great Commission, **(Matthew 28:20)** we are often anxious to respond to the needs within our safe and familiar territory but very reluctant to step beyond it in faith, to allow the Lord to have His own way with us. Moses protested and gave excuses, but the Lord assured him of His own grace and loving care. Some 40 years earlier, Moses had wanted to be the deliverer in his own strength and ended up running from Pharaoh like a coward. There are many people today that need deliverance from the chains of sin. Their deliverance can only be assured if we are willing to say "here am I, send me."

Zerubbabel had to step out of his comfort zone before he could lead the willing Jews back to Jerusalem. His life, that of the elders, and that of the people who followed him back to Jerusalem were in constant danger; but Zerubbabel's obedience to God triumphed all trials and tribulations. The deliverance of the people of God became a reality because there was a Zerubbabel who was opened to the stirring of the Spirit of God.

Proclaiming Christ To The Outcasts Of Society

When Zerubbabel obeyed the stirrings of the Holy Spirit to leave his comfort zone, it allowed him to minister to the needs of the weak and feeble Jews who had been left behind during the captivity. Those people were the outcasts in their own land. The people, who had been re-settled in the land of Israel by the Babylonian captors, treated the remaining Jews terribly. The Jews had no voice in their own land. All of this changed when Zerubbabel and his team arrived in Jerusalem.

In the book of Acts, we read of Peter, a Jew defying tradition and custom, and leaving his comfort zone to walk in obedience to God. Peter ministered to the Gentiles, the societal outcast of the day. When he got to the house of Cornelius, a Gentile, Peter said to them, **"Ye know how that it is an unlawful thing for a man that is a Jew to keep company, or come unto one of another nation, but God hath showed me that I should not call any man common or unclean"** **(Acts 10:28).** Peter responded to the stirring of the Spirit of God to step out of his comfort zone of cultural discrimination and prejudice to minister to Gentiles, and then brought them to Christ. When Peter preached of Christ to the Gentiles he saw the move of God and exclaimed, **"Of truth I perceive that God is no respecter of persons" (Acts 10:34).** Are we being held back by our denominational pride, self-centeredness and spiritual insecurities? Have we been so fed by the Lord that we cannot get up to do his will?

I am praying for the day when the people of God will come into agreement with John the Baptist's profound statement, **"He must increase, that I must decrease" (John, 3:30).** John appears to be saying, "I surrender my status and fame that they do not become hindrances to what God wants to do in my life and that of the people." Zerubbabel's leadership transcended race, tribes, and nationality. He ministered to the tribes of Judah and Benjamin and also ministered to the remaining Jews in the land and the nations around them who genuinely sought the God of Israel.

I am becoming increasingly convinced that the revival we've all longed for and prayed for is being delayed until the racial and cultural barriers are dissolved by the fire of the Holy

Ghost. There are signs in many quarters that the Lord is doing just that to pave the way for a deep, moving, and shaking revival before He returns for His bride.

Changing The World

The world is waiting for real spiritual and selfless world changers who walk in the anointing with demonstration of the power of the gospel to transform our world. Sad to say, many even within the church have turned their attention on "political messiahs" who speak and promise big things, which, if they are even able to deliver could not have lasting answers to the many troubling questions facing mankind. These political "geniuses" do not have the solutions to human depravity nor bring about a spiritual awakening and healing to our depraved world. This, I believe is the work of the Church.

The Greek word, ecclesia, meaning "the called out" signifies the setting apart of the church to impact the culture. This will require men and women of God to step out of their comfort zones into the unknown for the Holy Spirit to dictate the agenda to bring about changing our world for the Lord.

Israel at this time was almost a forgotten nation. It was probably out of the memories of many. It was almost off the map of the then world as a nation. Even some of the Jews in Persia had given up any hope of returning to the Promised Land. Zerubbabel's return to rebuild the temple put Israel back on the world map and literally changed the world. As the sacrifices and the various holy feasts were celebrated, they got the attention of all of the other nations.

The world had suddenly changed. The returning Jews and the remnant could now worship their God. For over 70 years the captives had not celebrated any of the holy feasts. For the first time they were able to celebrate those feasts in obedience to the word of the Lord, **"...as it is written in the Law of Moses the man of God" (Ezra 3:2).**

As the Church allows the Holy Spirit to stir her up, the dividing line between the pews and the streets of our world will dissipate and the lost will find room at the cross. Indeed, stepping out of our comfort zone into divine purpose changes the world. This was exactly the accusation of those who were resistant to the work of Paul and Silas when they declared, **"These that have turned the world upside down have come hither also" (Acts 17:6).** The accusers had seen a demonstration of the power of the gospel. In **Acts 8:5-8**, the Scripture also tells the story of Phillip, a deacon in the Church, who fled from Jerusalem during the great persecution for Samaria where he had ministered and changed the community with demonstrations of the power of the gospel.

Changing the world does not require a multitude of people or riches but rather a soul that is totally sold out to God. This was the case with Elijah on Mount Carmel where one man with God proved to be more than majority **(See I Kings 18).** David

Livingstone left Glasgow, Scotland for the "dark continent" of Africa to minister among natives who were often unfriendly. His work brought the light. The light which changed the way many of the natives viewed the world. Livingstone led many to the Lord and then died in Africa. Before carrying his body to the coast to be shipped back to Scotland, his native friends took out his heart and buried it under a tree saying, "This is where his heart is."

Livingstone was obedient to the heavenly calling, and also loved the people he ministered to by giving his life. Through Livingstone's work the English mindset that Africans had no concept of God was changed forever. This contributed to the great missionary thrust at the turn of the nineteenth century into Africa.

D. L. Moody responding to the stirring of the Holy Spirit left his job as a salesman and picked up his cross. His ministry took both America and England by storm. Today, many still talk about the Moody revival. It was indeed a world changing move of God.

Results For Obeying The Stirring Of The Holy Spirit

When Zerubbabel and the elders surrendered in obedience to the stirring of the Holy Spirit they were able to stir many of the Jews to follow them back to Jerusalem. The Scripture declares, **"Now these are the children of the province which went up out of the captivity, of those which had been carried away, when**

Nebuchadnezzar the king of Babylon had carried away unto Babylon, and came again unto Jerusalem and Judah, every man unto his own house, which came with Zerubbabel" (Ezra 2:1).

The obedience and zeal of the spiritual leadership in pursuing the things of God have the capacity to stir up the spirit of the people of God to follow. This was the greatest migration of the Jews from a strange land back to their home land after the Exodus. According to Scripture, about 50,000 people left Babylon to follow Zerubbabel and the elders to make the 700-mile journey to Jerusalem **(See Ezra 2:64 & 65).** When the leaders moved into new dimensions of spiritual living in Christ, the congregation also followed. By the examples of Zerubbabel and the elders, these Jews were willing to leave the place they had called home for over 70 years and all of the things they had grown accustomed, to step out in faith.

The faith of the church rises to a new level to believe in God for great things, when revival leaders step out by yielding to the leading of the Holy Spirit. We must remember that most of these Jews were born in Babylon and had never tasted the glorious heydays of Jerusalem. They had never experienced the days of Solomon's temple and its beautiful worship, the great palace, the peace and tranquility the nation of Israel enjoyed under Kings David and Solomon. Those were the days the temple worship was pure and the Word of the Lord was quite frequent through the prophets.

Most of them had only heard these stories and yet believed that their God was able to restore it all unto them. Like Jesus said, **"...blessed are they that have not seen, and yet have believed" (John 20:29).** When leaders surrender totally to the Lord it triggers an infectious phenomenon of faith upon the people to **".... walk by faith and not by sight." (II Thessalonians 5:17).**

The obedience to the stirring of the Holy Spirit gave the people the opportunity to recognize their God-given strength and power to withstand and defeat the forces of darkness. Outside the immediate protection of the Persian army, they were able to trust in their God to resist the attacks from their enemies **(See Ezra 5:1-5).**

By obeying the leading of the Lord to go back to Israel, Zerubbabel and the elders entered into intimacy with their God. Both their spiritual and their national identities were restored **(See Ezra 4:1-2; Ezra 6:20-22).** Zerubbabel's revival leadership moved the people into the place where God wanted them, when he and the elders surrendered to the stirring of the Spirit of God.

Chapter Three

Prayer: The Right Priority Of Revival Leadership

...the people gathered themselves together as one man to Jerusalem. Then stood up Jeshua the son of Jozadak, and his brethren the priests, and Zerubbabel and the son of Shealtiel, and his brethren, and builded the altar of the God of Israel, to offer burn offerings thereon, as it is written in the law of Moses the man of God. And they set the altar upon his bases; for fear was upon them because of the people of those countries; and they offered burn offerings thereon unto the Lord, even burn offerings morning and evening. **(Ezra 3:1-3).**

Zerubbabel identified the first and most important priority of his ministry; which was rebuilding the altar of The Most High God. Rebuilding the altar of the Lord represented a renewal of covenant and of faith in the Almighty. The altar symbolized a meeting place with God, a place to renew vision and strength, and a place to seek divine help and grace in times of crisis to continue the work to which they had been called. It is very important to note that alter building during the Old Testament times was, in most cases, necessary when seeking the Lord; as in the cases of Abraham **(Genesis 22)**, Jacob **(Genesis 28),** Elijah **(II Kings 18)** and Gideon **(Judges 6).**

In the New Testament church, this rebuilding of the altar represents the earnest and sincere prayer of faith of the believer. For us to develop an intimate relationship with the Lord and move into revival, our prayer life must be consistent, sincere and rooted in God's word. In **Jeremiah 33:3,** the Lord said, **"Call unto me, and I will answer thee, and show thee great and mighty things, which thou knowest not"**

God desires to fellowship with His people and reveal hidden truths to them. This is possible via prayer, reading and meditating on the Scripture. God has promised that He will open the curtains and show us the mysteries and hidden truths of which we do not know. By making altar building and prayer his top priority, Zerubbabel was positioning himself for divine favor in order to lead the people of God. Likewise, in the ministry of Jesus Christ, prayer was a top priority. Mark's gospel describes the importance of prayer in Jesus' ministry in these words, **"And in the morning**

rising up a great while before day, he went out, and departed into a solitary place, and there prayed" (Mark 1:35). If prayer was a top priority for the son of God, then it must be ours too, if we are to move into revival.

The Scriptures have many examples of individuals who sought the Lord in prayer and then changed their circumstances and the world around them **(see Acts 10; Acts 12).** The following will highlight the spiritual lessons that could be learned from Zerubbabel's leadership principle of making altar building (prayer) his first and foremost ministry priority.

Divine Principle Of Oneness

The scripture declares, "The people gathered themselves together as one man to Jerusalem" (Ezra 3:1). Zerubbabel, his elders and the people sensing the need to establish a place of meeting with God came together in one accord. Zerubbabel was able to bring the people together around a common purpose of meeting with Jehovah. Their coming together was neither for a church business meeting nor for any other purpose except to meet and do the will of the Lord. Uniting the church in prayer is the key to taking back what the enemy has stolen and repossessing our inheritance.

Revival leadership inspires a unified presence and purpose to seek the Lord. Apostle Paul, in challenging the believers at Philippi to unify with a common purpose wrote, **"Only let your** conversation be as it becomes the gospel of Jesus Christ, that whether I come and see you, or else be absent, I may hear of your affairs, that ye stand fast in one spirit with one mind, striving together for the faith of the gospel" (Philippians 1: 27).** Zerubbabel was able to unite the people to stand together in the face of strong opposition. Similarly, King Jehoshaphat applied a strategy of uniting the people when they were threatened by combined enemy forces.

The Scriptures declare that Jehoshaphat's ability in uniting the people to seek the Lord brought them a magnificent victory. The Scripture states, **"And Judah gathered themselves together to seek help of the Lord: even out of all the cities of Judah they came to seek the Lord" (II Chronicles, 20:2; also see verses 20-24; I Kings 18: 30-39).** When the people are united in prayer, there is a release of divine outpouring.

This was also the case with the early church. The church was able to march forward in a great movement of the Spirit because it was in "one accord." This theme of "one accord" is evident throughout the book of Acts. Jesus made the importance of unity in the body even more clear when approaching the throne of God.

Jesus stated, **"Again I say unto you, that if two of you shall agree on earth as touching anything that they shall ask, it shall be done for them of my father which is in heaven. For where two or three are gathered together in my name, there I am in the midst of them" (Matthew 18:19&20).**

It is important that individual members of the body, the pastor and the leaders pray. However, there is a greater release of power when a revival leader is able to bring the church into unity in prayer (See **Acts 2:1-4; Acts 4:23-31**). The old adage "united we stand, divided we fall" is indeed applicable to the prayer life of the church of Jesus Christ , who admonished the church to be one as He and the Father are one. A divided church is an easy prey in the jaws of Satan and his demons. It is like placing a sign in front of the church that states, "Demons welcome; no password needed."

Divine Principle Of Obedience

Zerubbabel was a leader who followed the Word of God. Zerubbabel and the elders established prayer or renewed their covenant relationship by building the altar of sacrifice in accordance with the Word of God, **"...as is written in the law of Moses, the man of God" (Ezra 3:2)**. Individual opinions and ideas were not a consideration. Because the returning Jews based every action on the Lord's Word, neither doctrinal nor theological conflicts held them back from doing what the Lord had called them to do. Working in accordance with God's Word had brought them into the arena of total obedience. The revival leader must be able to bring the people of God into obedience around a common denominator, which is "Thus says the Lord." Such obedience cannot come through philosophy, ideology or a denominational distinctive. Obedience is only possible through the leadership's visible practice and their private obedience to the Word of the Lord.

The revival leader must always remember that one of the enemy's strategies to hinder or disrupt revival is stirring up confusion that leads to disobedience among the people of God. Apostle Paul admonished the Thessalonians, saying **"pray without ceasing... for this is the will of God in Christ Jesus concerning you" (1 Thessalonians 5:17&18).** The Lord, at his darkest moment said to the disciples, **"... Pray that ye enter not into temptation" (Luke 22:40).**

The obedience on the part of Zerubbabel and the people kept them from falling into the enemy's trap which could have hindered their efforts to rebuild the temple. King Saul fell into the enemy's trap when he disobeyed the divine directive to destroy the Amalekites. The Lord's displeasure at King Saul's disobedience was expressed through the prophet Samuel this way, **"...Behold to obey is better than sacrifice... For rebellion is as the sin of witchcraft, and stubbornness as iniquity and idolatry. Because thou hast rejected the word of the Lord, he hath also rejected thee from being king" (1 Samuel 15:22&23).** It is possible that Zerubbabel had King Saul's episode in the back of his mind. King Saul's disobedience cost him the throne. On the other hand, the obedience of the church to act in accordance with the Word of the Lord will destine her for the throne.

The prophet Elijah on Mount Carmel against the forces of Baal said this in the prayer that brought down the fire from heaven to consume the sacrifice, **"...I am thy servant, and that I have done all these things at thy word." (2 Kings 18:36).** Just as Elijah's obedience to the Word of the Lord opened the heavens, so also Zerubbabel's obedience to the Lord ushered them into a new arena of a closer relationship with the God of Israel, whose sacrifices they had abandoned for over 70 years.

Release Of Power And Strength In The Face Of Satanic Resistance

One of Satan's fears is that the church of Jesus Christ is on fire for HIM. When the church is in obedience to and dependent on the Lord, hell is shaken. This is because the power of God is released upon the church to do exploits for the Kingdom of God. Therefore, it comes as no surprise that Satan mounts his fiercest attacks at every attempt and efforts towards revival. Zerubbabel's efforts were confronted by the enemy's unrelenting attacks that brought great fear upon them. **Ezra 3:3** states, **"And they set the altar upon his bases; for fear was upon them because of the people of the countries; and they offered burnt offerings thereon unto the Lord..."** The revival leader must always remember that the key to overcoming the enemy's resistance is to rebuild the altar of prayer.

Knowing full well that they were under attack and likely

to be attacked again, Zerubbabel moved forward into rebuilding the altar of sacrifice and prayer. It was quite clear to him and to the elders that they needed to look to their God for deliverance. Starting with prayer strengthened their faith and gave them the spiritual vitality to pursue the work to which the Lord had called them. As the church goes on her knees in prayer, the powers of darkness are not just shaken but also brought in subjection to the Lordship of our God. This is why prayer or the rebuilding of the altar draws Satan's fiercest attacks. Revival requires a deep, soaking, intense prayer firmly rooted and grounded in the Word of God.

The revival leader must give consideration to one thing and one thing alone: prayer in the face of the enemy's attack. King Jehoshaphat quickly turned to the Lord as his first and foremost strategy when he was informed of the approaching enemy. The Scriptures put it this way, **"Then there came some that told Jehoshaphat, saying, there comes a great multitude against thee... And Jehoshaphat feared, and set himself to seek the Lord, and proclaimed a fast throughout Judah" (II Chronicles 20:2&3).**

Rebuilding the altar was a powerful statement to the pagan nations who inhabited the land after the people of Israel had been taken into exile. It was a statement that Zerubbabel and the Jews had returned to take back what the enemy had stolen. It was also a statement to those inhabitants that the God of Israel is greater than their gods which were made of stone and wood.

During the time of the Judges, Gideon was told by the angel of the Lord to destroy the altar of Baal and build an altar to Him in its place. The Scripture declares it this way:

> **And it came to pass the same night, that the LORD said unto him, Take thy father's young bullock, even the second bullock of seven years old, and throw down the altar of Baal that thy father hath, and cut down the grove that is by it: And build an altar unto the LORD thy God upon the top of this rock, in the ordered place, and take the second bullock, and offer a burnt sacrifice with the wood of the grove which thou shalt cut down. Then Gideon took ten men of his servants, and did as the LORD had said unto him: and so it was, because he feared his father's household, and the men of the city, that he could not do it by day, that he did it by night. And when the men of the city arose early in the morning, behold, the altar of Baal was cast down, and the grove was cut down that was by it, and the second bullock was offered upon the altar that was built. And they said one to another, Who hath done this thing? And when they enquired and asked, they said, Gideon the son of Joash hath done this thing. Then the men**

of the city said unto Joash, Bring out thy son, that he may die: because he hath cast down the altar of Baal, and because he hath cut down the grove that was by it" (Judges 6:25 - 30).**

This move by Gideon triggered the anger of the people because Gideon's action was a statement to them that their gods were nothing in comparison to the true and the living God. The Lord affirmed his superiority over all other gods this way, **"Look unto me, and be ye saved, all the ends of the earth; for I am God, and there is none else" (Isaiah 45:22; also see Deut. 4:35 & 39; I Samuel 2:2; I Kings 8:60 II Chronicles 17; 20)**

Zerubbabel's actions should remind the church and all revival leaders that rebuilding the altar of the Lord or rebuilding prayer is an indication of a covenant relationship with the God of Heaven, the God who is greater and mightier than all other gods. The six very powerful words in the faith walk are "I have a covenant with God." This statement increases our faith, enhances our motivation to stand for the Lord, and to walk in obedience to His Lordship. It is a reminder of our source of hope and strength in times of crisis. Faith gives the believer a glorious hope for the present and the future. It is this realization that strengthened the hands and the convictions of Zerubbabel and the returning Jews to muster the hope and courage to rebuild the altar of sacrifices and the Temple of The Most High Lord.

Chapter Four

Putting Faith Into Action

They kept also the feast of tabernacles, as it is written, and all the set feasts of the Lord that were consecrated, and of everyone that willingly offered a freewill offering unto the Lord. From the first of the seventh month began they to offer burn offering unto the Lord. But the foundation of the temple of the Lord was not yet laid. **(Ezra 3:4 - 6)**

Zerubbabel and the Jews had not celebrated any of the appointed feasts in over 70 years. Their years in captivity had deprived them of the privilege of serving their God according to divine order. In fact, they had a localized perspective of their God, believing that He could only be worshipped in Jerusalem. According to the Psalmist, this was the Jew's response to their Babylonian captors when they were asked to sing some of the songs of Zion, **"There they that had carried us captive required us of a song, and they that wasted us required of us mirth, saying sing us one of the songs of Zion. How shall we sing the Lord's song in a strange land?" (Psalm 137:3&4).** In **Numbers 29:15-24**, the Lord has spelled out the appointed feasts and how and when they should be celebrated. During their years in captivity, the children of Israel had not observed these feasts, and most of the younger generation had not even experienced them. This was a period of spiritual famine in their history. The covenant relationship with the Lord had been strained by their lack of compliance with the appointed feasts.

Their life in bondage had made many of them complacent, settling for the customs and culture of their captors to the neglect of the Divine Order. Many of the returning Jews were born in captivity. Most of them had no knowledge of the appointed feast and the conditions necessary for their celebration. The Feast of Tabernacles, like many other appointed feasts, had not been celebrated in over 70 years. The spiritual benefits of celebrating the feasts were missing in their state of spiritual apostasy.

In many denominational circles today, the church has compromised the teachings and ordinances of the Lord. Like in the times of Emperor Constantine, the world has entered and influenced the church. With many in the pulpits adopting the appeasement approach, the church is becoming more like the world just as the world is becoming more like the church. The differences between the church and the world are hardly clear. In this kind of environment, the church compromises rather than striving together for the faith of the gospel of Jesus Christ **(see Philippians 1:27).** In revival times, a faithful leadership like that of Zerubbabel is needed to bring the church back to God's ordinances, and to help her walk in truth and obedience.

Conditions Necessary For The Celebration Of The Feast

Like most of the Jewish feasts, the Feast of Tabernacles was an agricultural feast, celebrated after harvest. The celebration meant that the returning Jews had sowed and harvested their crops. In this case though, they had no harvest because they had not sown; and therefore had nothing to celebrate. Thus, conditions were unfavorable for such celebration.

Moreover, the feast was to be celebrated with various activities within the temple. Zerubbabel and the Jews returned to a country that was desolate. The walls of the city of Jerusalem had been broken and burnt down. The temple of the Lord had been destroyed by their Babylonian captors. There was no temple in which to celebrate the feast.

The temple worship instituted after **"...the ordinance of David the King of Israel" (Ezra 4:10)** had diminished during their years in captivity. This worship was necessary for the celebration of the Feast of Tabernacles. The priesthood and the

Levitical singers had not been set in their place for the worship. Humanly speaking, there was nothing around them that gave any hope for the celebration of the feast. They had come to the end of their human capacities.

This is when faith begins. Like their father Abraham, not knowing where and how the promises would come to pass, the Jews stepped out in faith, believing that the God of their fathers was able to see them through. The author of the book of Hebrews put it this way, **"By faith Abraham when he was called out to go unto a place which he should later receive for an inheritance, obeyed; and he went out knowing whither he went" (Hebrews 11:8).** It was now their turns to walk and act in faith like their father Abraham.

The Faith Act

Acting in faith, the returning Jews celebrated the feasts they had neglected for over 70 years. The Scripture declares, **"They kept also the feast of tabernacles, as it is written, and offered the daily burnt offerings by number, according to the custom, as the duty of everyday required" (Ezra 3:4).** Even though the returning Jews had no harvest, no temple and no organized worship after the ordinance of David, Zerubbabel was able to move them from faith into manifestation. He was able to create a vision for the people to celebrate the Feast of Tabernacles even though the conditions on the ground indicated otherwise. As a revival leader, Zerubbabel was able to lead the people to walk by faith and not by sight **(See II Corinthians 5:7)**. Zerubbabel did not focus on what they did or did not have. Zerubbabel did not depend on what he could see but trusted the Lord who had called them to do His work.

The revival leader must be able to move the church into total dependence on Jesus Christ and not on the government, nor the circumstance around them. Our God is greater than our circumstances. The prevailing socio-economic and political climate may be challenging, but the Body of Christ must look beyond the immediate circumstances and unto the One who has promised to supply all of our needs and to be with us till the end of the age **(See Philippians 4:17 and Matthew 28:20)**. The songwriter penned it quite well this way:

My hope is built on nothing less,
But Jesus' blood and righteousness…
On Christ the Solid Rock, I stand,
All other grounds are sinking sound.

Zerubbabel and the returning Jews knew that their God was able and dependable. They knew that God would see them through and would never fail them. The same God is alive and well today and will see the church through if we will put our faith, trust and confidence in Him. All things are possible if only we will believe **(see Matthew 19:26)**. All the missing pieces are enough to discourage and dampen the faith of anybody. These kinds of situations have the potential to present leaders with all the excuses to complain and even to give up. Under such circumstances, believers may be tempted to focus on the challenges around them rather than on the Lord, their God. God is more than enough. When the faith of leaders and believers are dampened, they tend to spend their time talking about the problems and challenges facing them rather than rebuking them. The Lord gave the church a mandate to speak to the mountains in faith **(Mark, 11:23).**

Zerubbabel as a revival leader turned his back on all the negatives and focused on the one true God who called him into leading His people. Zerubbabel and the returning Jews spoke in faith and walked in faith instead of by what their eyes could see. The Scripture declares, **"From the first day of the seventh month began they to offer burnt offerings unto the Lord. But the foundation of the temple of the Lord was not yet laid"** **(Ezra 3:6).**

Zerubbabel was able to lead the returning Jews on a faith walk into celebrating the Feast of Tabernacles despite the absence of a temple foundation let alone the temple itself. The Zerubbabel slogan for revival leadership could have been something like "not what we cannot do, but what our God can do."

A revival leader must be able to move the people into realizing that it is not what they can do for God, but what God is able to do through them that matters most. The God whom

Zerubbabel served made it possible for him and the returning Jews to renew their covenant relationship by setting up the altar to offer the ordained sacrifices which had been neglected in their Babylonian captivity. This new spiritual experience stirred them to serve the Lord with their lives and also with everything else that the Lord had blessed them with.

Faith To Invest In The Kingdom Of God

When revival leaders are able to move the people of God into walking by faith, deeper faith is stirred within God's people that they are willing to invest in the things of God. After celebrating the Feast of Tabernacles without a temple, the returning Jews were stirred in their spirits to give towards the construction of a new temple. They had experienced the blessings of the Feast of Tabernacles; stirring such deep faith within them, that they were willing to serve the Lord their God with their lives and substance. The Scripture says, **"They gave money also unto the masons, and the carpenters…" (Ezra 3:7).** They were ready to see the Temple built.

There was no special fundraising program, nor any long emotional stirring or manipulative tactics which sadly have become a common place in some quarters of the church today. Instead, it was a genuine realization of what could happen when they put their faith in their God that motivated the returning Jews to freely and cheerfully give towards the reconstruction of the temple. Blessings follow this kind of giving. If the church today is experiencing a lack, there must be a problem with the kind of faith the leadership is portraying and moving the congregations into.

Chapter Five

Laying A Sound Foundation In Revival Times

And when the builders had laid the foundation of the temple of the Lord, they set the priests in their apparel with trumpets, and the Levites the sons of Asaph with cymbals, to praise the Lord, after the ordinance of David the King of Israel. And they sang together by chorus in praising and giving thanks to the Lord. And all the people shouted with a great shout, when they praised the Lord, because the foundation of the house of the Lord was laid. **(Ezra 3:10&11)**

Zerubbabel had given the returning Jews a taste of blessings from the Lord through the celebration of the Feast of Tabernacles; a blessing which many of them had never experienced. They had then joyfully given towards the reconstruction of the temple. Many of the 50,000 returning Jews were born in captivity in Babylon and neither saw the magnificent temple of Solomon nor ever experienced temple worship. As a result, they could not imagine what the temple would look like. As a revival leader, Zerubbabel had the task of leading the people in laying a solid foundation for the temple. Laying a foundation for a building is a challenging task. However, with his great leadership skills, Zerubbabel was able to make the foundation building a glorious moment and it gave the people a vision of the temple that such a great foundation could prepare them for. The floor plan for the foundation gave the returning Jews, especially the younger generation who never saw the first temple, an expectation of greater things to come. The anticipation of temple worship might even have been so spiritually uplifting, that they could not help but to jump into celebration, when the foundation of the house of the Lord was laid.

Laying a sound foundation in revival times is of paramount importance for stability and sustainability. Many revivals have ended abruptly and sometimes sadly because the people focused on their emotions rather than the Scriptures for direction and stability. It is tempting to focus on experiences and even turn them into doctrine rather than the teachings of Scripture. Replacing the teachings of the bible with emotional experiences is a recipe for cult worship and for confusion that could bring about an abrupt end to revival. However, emotions are a part of the human experience during revival times and are not always harmful if guided by Scripture, rather than taking the place of the scriptural doctrines.

The early church had great emotional experiences with the first-ever New Testament outpouring of the Holy Ghost. Signs and wonders were everywhere. It was a daily experience of the church. However, the direction of the revival was rooted and grounded in the word of God. The Scripture declares, **"And they continued steadfastly in the apostles' doctrine and in fellowship, and in breaking of bread and in prayers" (Acts 2:42).** This was the focus despite their great emotional experiences. It was this focus on the word of God and obedience to the leading of the Holy Spirit that sustained the revival of those days. This was the foundation for the sustained revival of the early church that enabled them to deal with doctrinal conflicts **(See Acts, 15)** and to weed out corruption from their midst **(See Acts, 5).**

In the life of the returning Jews, rebuilding the temple was of great importance to their worship. Celebrating the various appointed feasts, the Davidic worship and the priestly activities all made the rebuilding of the temple a necessity. A temple built to last, required a foundation that could sustain both the structure and the activities that would be carried out within it; but a foundation does not tell of the beauty of the end product. A foundation is not an attractive feature of a building. However, a strong foundation gives an indication of the stability of the building. A strong foundation in revival times determines the sustainability of the revival. Thus Zerubbabel made this a priority.

Like any structure, revival must have a firm foundation to ensure its biblical integrity and spiritual relevance to the church in particular, and to the world as a whole. A revival leader must be able to turn this arduous task into a celebration by giving the people of God a vision of what a strong foundation will prepare them for. If such a foundation is destroyed or damaged then the church and its revival could be put in disarray. The Psalmist affirmed this when he asked, **"If the foundation be destroyed, what will the righteous do?" (Psalm 11:3).**

Many great revival leaders have come on the world scene, but many such as Jimmy Swaggart and Jim Bakker of the Praise The Lord Club (PTL) eventually went down in disgrace because of the lack of biblical, moral and financial integrity. In fact, the faith of many believers was shaken and some even left the faith when Jimmy Swaggart and Jim Baker fell. It is apparent that the longevity and strength of a revival and its leadership is dependent on the foundation upon which they build.

Apostle Paul emphasizing the importance of the foundation stated, **"For other foundation can no man lay than that is laid, which is Jesus Christ." (I Corinthian 3:11).** Paul is pointing out to the Corinthians that the foundation the church must build on is none other than the Lord Jesus Christ. Jesus is the rock of Gibraltar and the rock of ages. He is the rejected stone that became the head stone of the corner **(Matthew 21:42).** Thus the foundation for stable and sustained revival is nothing else but Christ alone and his teachings.

Building A Foundation In The Natural

Humanly speaking, building a foundation is a challenging task. Requiring careful planning, a builder must follow the specifications of the building floor plan to ensure that the foundation is dug to the right depth and width. This task involves digging out all unacceptable rocks and debris to make way for the concrete, the stones and the steel rods that are needed for the foundation. It is this foundation that shores up the final structure against storms and heavy winds.

The foundation of a building is not attractive. Generally people talk about beautiful buildings and not "beautiful" foundations. Though unseen, unrecognized and often times unappreciated by the average person, it is the foundation that holds the building firmly in place. Likening those who hear and do what He teaches to a strong and firm house, Jesus stated, **"He is like a man which build a house, and dug deep, and laid the foundation on a rock, and when the flood arose, the stream beat vehemently upon the house, and could not shake it: for it was founded upon a rock" (Luke 6:48).**

Just as a building needs a firm foundation to withstand the

heavy winds and storms, a revival needs sound biblical teachings with all decisions rooted and grounded in the Scripture to avoid false teachings, humanistic philosophies, and the conflicts that have plagued many revival leaders and churches. Zerubbabel and the returning Jews knew the importance of a firm foundation. A weak foundation would lead to serious problems in the long run. Jesus again likened those who heard his teachings but refused to obey them to a house built on a poor foundation this way, "**... is like a man that without a foundation built a house upon the earth; against which the streams did beat vehemently, and immediately it fell; and the ruin of that house was great**"(Luke 6:49).

A poor foundation will fail a housing inspection and be denied the permit to continue building because such a house is dangerous for habitation. Likewise, revival without strong biblical and spiritual integrity could pose a serious danger to the people of God, such as the ordination of homosexuals into the ministry, high divorce rate in the church, and even many evangelicals seeing the Great Commission as a thing of the past.

Zerubbabel as a revival leader understood that if he was going to lead in the rebuilding of a temple to the almighty God, he had to make sure that it was built to last. The Jews had returned to stay for good. They were not on a temporary or a short term mission. They had returned to retake their inheritance and re-establish the worship of their God, which had been neglected for over 70 years. The Jews were aiming for a permanent building that could sustain their way of worship. As a result, they ordered all the necessary building materials for the reconstruction efforts towards a strong foundation and a solid structure.

The Scripture declares, **"And they gave money also unto the masons and the carpenters, and to them of Tyre to bring cedar trees from Lebanon to the sea of Joppa, according to the grant that they had of Cyrus king of Persia" (Ezra 3:7)**. Revival leadership must aim at sustained revival and not that which is unstable and filled with faulty teachings and mere emotionalism. Unsustained revival has the potential of causing the people of God to become lukewarm and complacent in their faith.

The completion of the foundation stirred different emotions. The ancient among them who saw Solomon's temple wept because they could not tell what the new temple would look like from the foundation. The younger generation who had only heard of Solomon's temple shouted praises because they anticipated seeing a glorious temple upon the foundation **(See Ezra 4:12&13)**.

No one could tell what the temple would look like from the foundation, yet Zerubbabel was able to turn it into a joyful celebration. As a strong spiritual and disciplined leader, Zerubbabel led with faith and with conviction about what God was able to do with them, through them and for them rather than what they could do.

Foundation Building In The Spiritual Sense

In the spiritual sense it must be noted that Zerubbabel and the returned Jews based their actions on prayer and on the word of their God. This is evident from Ezra's account that they **"...built the altar of the God of Israel to offer burnt offerings thereon, as it is written in the law of Moses the man of God" (Ezra 3:2).** The laying of the foundation was of a great spiritual significance to the returning Jews. It was the foundation for the temple which was the center of worship of their God. To Zerubbabel, laying a strong spiritual foundation was an indication of great things to come. It gave an indication of the strength and stability of the structure that would be built upon it. As in the words of Oral Roberts, *"something good is going to happen."* Spiritual foundation requires specific spiritual stones to strengthen it. There are many precious spiritual stones for a strong spiritual foundation in revival times. However, this volume is not aimed at an exhaustive study of these stones. The following are just a few of the precious stones necessary in revival times for growth and sustainability:

A) **Faith**

Zerubbabel was a man of faith. He firmly believed in the prophecies concerning their return to Jerusalem after 70 years in captivity and the rebuilding of the temple. His faith as a revival leader was based on the word of God as predicted by Jeremiah and Isaiah **(See Jeremiah 29:10-14; Isaiah 44:28; Isaiah 45:13).** Indeed faith comes by hearing the word of God **(See Romans**

10:17). His conviction that the Lord would lead them back home to rebuild the temple was not based on feelings or humanistic ideas or on traditions and philosophy or on church distinctive. It was solely based on their faith in God and His word. By their faith they had positioned themselves to be pleasing to God as declared in Scripture that, **"Without faith it is impossible to please God; for he that comes to God must believe that he is, and that he is a rewarded of those who diligently seek him"** (Hebrews **11:6).** A revival leader must believe not just a portion of, but the entire Word of God, the Bible. For it provides the church and its leadership with doctrine, reproof, correction and instruction to stay the course **(See II Timothy 3:16).** God is not moved by our tears nor our circumstances but rather our faith. Lack of faith can hinder the move of the Spirit and the onward march of the church. Jesus said that if we have faith and do not doubt in our hearts we can command the stumbling blocks in our lives and ministries to be removed **(See Mark 11: 23-24).**

With the priests around him, Zerubbabel was fully exposed to the word. His knowledge and understanding of the word had increased his faith in the God of Israel. Revival rooted and grounded in faith in Christ has lasting impact just as it was with the revival of the early church as recorded in the book of Acts.

B) Prayer

Zerubbabel's leadership was saturated with prayer. His first ministry priority upon coming back to Jerusalem was the rebuilding of God's alter, which had been destroyed. This altar building symbolized prayer. There has never been a revival without prayer.

During the dedication of the first temple, Solomon prayed and God's glory came upon them. The Scripture declares,

"Now when Solomon has made an end to praying, the fire came down from heaven and consumed the burnt offering and the sacrifices: and the glory of the Lord filled the house. And the priests could not enter into the house of the Lord, because the glory of the Lord had filled the Lord's house" (II Chronicles 7:1&2). The whole congregation of Israel was in unity and total agreement as Solomon offered the prayer.

God's glory descends and revival occurs when the people of God get down to pray. This is more than just a couple of leaders praying during the Sunday services. It requires the dedicated prayer life of the entire church. A church with a burden for prayer, and set themselves to pray together as a body is a praying church.

Every born-again believer has the Bible right to pray and expect results. Jesus put it this way, **"…and I say not unto you that I will pray the father for you, for the father himself knows you because you have loved me and have believed that I came from God" (John 16:26&27).** Jesus is telling the disciples that the Father knows them. Therefore, they have every right to approach the throne of grace, and God will answer them. He made it very clear to them that they had to do the praying as He was going to the Father.

Every believer is known by the Father and has the right to approach the Father in prayer. "All hands on deck" to pray is an absolute essential for revival. Paul told the Thessalonians to **"pray without ceasing." (I Thessalonians, 5:17).** Paul is simply stating the obvious; we should never stop praying. This was a very important matter to Paul as we consider his teachings on spiritual warfare in his epistle to the Ephesians. After telling his audience about the various pieces of the amour for spiritual warfare, Paul ended by saying, **"Praying always with all prayer and supplication in the spirit, and watching thereunto with all perseverance and supplication for all the saints, and for me also that utterance may be given to me to boldly make known the mystery of the gospel" (Ephesians 6:18&19).** All the pieces of the armor are designed for face-to-face combat. Prayer, however, is for face-to-face combat as well as for long range attacks on the enemy. Serving as an inter-continental missile, prayer reaches the entire human race on every corner of the universe. Prayer knows no bounds.

The church may have all the pieces of the spiritual armor, yet without prayer, the pieces of the armor may not be very effective. There is indeed power in prayer. Something supernatural happens when the church prays. The song writer put it this way:

Lord listen to your children praying,
Lord send your spirit in the place,
Lord listen to your children praying,

Send us love, send us power, and send us grace
Something gonna happen as the world has never known,
When the children of the Lord get down to pray.

The Lord admonished the disciples about the urgency of prayer saying, **"...rise and pray, lest you enter into temptation" (See Luke 22:46).** Hannah prayed with urgency and the Lord opened her womb to have a son who brought the people of Israel back to the true worship of God **(See I Samuel 1:9-2:11).** Jehoshaphat prayed when his enemies joined together to attack Judah and God gave him a great victory **(See II Chronicles, 20).** In the midst of the early church's revival, the church had to pray to stop the onslaught of the saints **(See Acts 12: 5- 11).**

The great Scottish preacher, John Knox, praying with a deep sense of urgency for revival, cried out to God, saying, *"***Give me Scotland or I die.***"* The impact of the revival that grew out of his prayer is still with us today.

God's will is for His church to stay fervent and alive in prayer. When the people of God are on their knees, hell is subdued and revival is released. When I was teaching at the Liberia Theological Institute, there was a slogan on the wall that read, **"Theology Without Kneelogy is Powerless."** This was to be a reminder to the students and faculty alike that while they study theology, they should also spend time on their knees in prayer. It is unfortunately estimated that an average pastor in the United

States prays just 30 minutes a day. This explains why the church appears to be losing her influence in the society. A revival leader needs to feed daily on the Word, but must also see prayer like the blood that flows through his or her spiritual veins to keep him or her alive and fervent in the spirit. However, prayer is one thing that is done less and less in the church today.

C) Unity Of The Body

Unity is a very important building block for stability in revival times. Revival does not thrive in an environment of confusion and internal squabbles. Zerubbabel and the returning Jews were united in their efforts to lay the foundation for the temple. In their preparation to work on the foundation, **"the people gathered themselves together as one man to Jerusalem." (Ezra 3:1).** They were focused with a singular purpose of rebuilding the altar of sacrifices and laying the foundation for the temple of their God. There was no room for doctrinal or denominational differences which has sadly divided the body of Christ throughout the centuries. Prior to the first New Testament outpouring of the Holy Ghost the Scripture states, **"And when the day of Pentecost was fully come, they were all with one accord in one place" (Acts 2:1).**

The hearts of the people of God are joined together as, it becomes like a platform upon which the Holy Spirit stands to manifest the presence of the Lord in His church; for where two or three are gathered in his name, there he is in their midst **(see Matthew 18:20)**. In his effort to keep the Philippians united in their pursuit of the things of God, Apostle Paul wrote, **"Only let your conversation be as it becomes the gospel of Christ, that whether I come again to see you, or else be absent, I may hear of your affairs that ye stand fast in one mind, with one spirit, striving together for the faith of the gospel"** (Philippians 1:27; See also Philippians 2:2&3, Romans 15:5&6 Ephesians 4:1-13).

When the body of Christ is united, it affords each person in the body the opportunity to bless and be blessed by others. With diversities of spiritual gifts within the body, each person is spiritually nourished to grow in the grace and knowledge of the Lord. **(See Romans 12:3)**. Like the human body all the parts work in harmony to make the body whole. If one part is not functioning properly the whole body is affected. This kind of unity will help keep the revival alive and prevent satanic infiltrations. The Psalmist summed up the benefits of unity in revival times this way;

"Behold, how good and how pleasant *it is* for brethren to dwell together in unity! It is like the precious oil upon the head, Running down on the beard, The beard of Aaron, Running down on the edge of his garments. It is like the dew of Hermon, Descending upon the mountains of Zion; For there the LORD commanded the blessing. Life forevermore" (Psalm 133:1-3). This Psalm is admonishing The Church to put all our differences behind us and join together as brothers and sisters with a singular purpose of serving the Lord.

D) The Cross

The altar of sacrifices was the ministry priority of Zerubbabel and the returning Jews. Building the altar was very significant because it symbolized a renewal of covenant relationship with their God. It is this covenant relationship that strengthened and encouraged them in their pursuit of the things of God. Even in the face of the challenges posed by their enemies, they were willing to pay the price. The altar represents the cross of Christ. This was where the sin offerings and all the blood sacrifices were made.

Zerubbabel was very diligent in his obedience to the Law of Moses, the man of God **(Ezra 4:2)** in making sure that the ordained blood sacrifices were re-instituted. It was on the way to an altar of sacrifice on mount Moriah, when Abraham prophesied to his son Isaac that God will provide himself a lamb for a burnt offering **(Genesis 22:8)**. On the mount God provided a ram in the stead of Isaac. Christ's death on the cross was the fulfillment of **"God will provide himself a lamb for a burnt offering" (Genesis 22:8)**. The death of Christ on the cross is the ultimate blood sacrifices for the sins of the whole world. It was at the cross that the Son of God gave it all that we may have life in abundance **(See John 10:10)**.

The cross is a reminder to the believer that there is a race that must be ran and a price that must be paid. It symbolizes the call to the kind of commitment that is expected of the believer.

The Church is not called unto self preservation, but rather to self sacrifice for the sake of the gospel. Jesus put it this way, **"if any man will come after me, let him deny himself, and take his cross and follow me: For whosoever will save his life shall lose it, but whosoever shall lose his life for my sake shall find it" (Matthew 16:24&25; See also Mark 8:34&35).** If the church is to experience and sustain revival, we must understand that we are called to a total commitment and not just to make contributions or do things only when it is convenient.

It is out of such great commitment that victory will come forth. The Lord after listening to the rich young ruler's list of his good deeds said to him, **"One thing thou lackest, go thy way, sell whatsoever things thou have, and give to the poor, and thou shall have treasures in heaven, and come, take up thy cross, and follow me"**

(Mark 10:20). The cross is a symbol of offense and shame to the world yet it is the only way to redemption **(See Galatians 5:11).**

Encouraging the Corinthian church to stand firm for the preaching of the cross despite the shame and persecution attached to it, Paul wrote, **"For the preaching of the cross is unto them that perish foolishness, but unto us which are saved it is the power of God" (I Corinthians 1:18).** It is not something of beauty. The mentioning of Christ and His cross make people angry, yet it is that cross which the church is called to bear. Apostle Paul expressed his own dedication to the cross this way, " **But God forbid that I should glory save in the cross of our Lord Jesus Christ…"(Galatians 6:14).** He again stated, **"From henceforth let no man trouble me, for I bear in my body the marks of the Lord Jesus" (Galatians 6:17).**

The bearing of the cross is the highest calling of God to the church. A symbol of great commitment, the cross is an important foundation for revival. In his hymn, emphasizing the church's glorious victory that will result from dedication and total commitment to the cross, Daniel Bernard wrote:

So I'll cherish the old rugged cross,
Till my trophies at last I lay down;
I will cling to the old rugged cross,
And exchange it someday for a crown.

"The Old Rugged Cross" is a hymn that always brings tears of joy to my eyes. This was the favorite hymn of my father J. B. Amankwatia, who went home to be with the Lord in 1995. In one of his last statements to me, he reminded me that this hymn was his life's focus and purpose. In his usual sweet and loving voice, Daddy remarked, "Son, cling tight to the cross with all your heart and never let go." Indeed it continues to shape my life and ministry today. It is Christ's death on the cross and his resurrection that the church is commanded to bear witness to throughout the world **(Mark, 16:15).**

E) Urgency Of The Great Commission

The Great Commission, **"Go ye into all the earth and preach the gospel to every creature"(Mark 16:15)**, is an almost a forgotten or neglected mandate of the church. We often state the seven words of the "dying" Christ on the cross during Good Friday services. We are taught these seven words in Sunday school as children. These words are very important reminders of the price Christ paid for the sins of the world. However, we hardly hear of the words of the "risen" Christ. There are many church goers who do not know the words of the "risen" Christ.

When Jesus showed himself to his disciples after his resurrection he said to them, **"Peace be unto you: as my father has sent me even so send I you" (John 20:21; See also Matthew 28:18-20).** He was sending the disciples to reach the world with the gospel (His death and resurrection) just as the Father sent him to do. The Great Commission is the heartbeat of God. The only way the world will come to a saving faith in the Lord is when they hear the gospel preached and taught.

Apostle Paul clarified it this way, **"For whosoever shall call upon the name of the Lord shall be saved. How then shall they call on him in whom they have not believed? And how shall they believe on him of whom they have not heard? And how shall they hear without a preacher?" (Romans 10:13&14).** In order for the world to believe the gospel, people must first hear it and believe; as the scripture declares, **"So then faith cometh by hearing, and hearing by the work of God" (See Romans 10:17).**

In 2003, I attended a mission's service in Tampa, Florida when a beautiful young woman serving as a missionary in India shared a heart wrenching testimony of a Hindu couple who threw their newborn into the river Ganges as a sacrifice to their Hindu god. She mentioned that she and her colleagues were a distance away when they saw the couple throw their newborn into the river. When they arrived at the scene, they began to share the gospel with the couple. Afterwards, the mother of the baby turned to them in tears and said, "Why did you come so late? If you had been here sooner my baby would not have died. I would still be holding her in my arms." How many such missed opportunities are out there in our homes, families, churches, towns, cities, countries and the continents of the world?

In order for the church not to miss such opportunities a preacher or someone must take the gospel out into the world. If the church is not fulfilling the Great Commission, there is no guarantee that many will be won to Christ. When the church steps out into the world to share the good news of the kingdom the Lord is glorified, and the church is blessed. The prophet Isaiah put it this way, **"How beautiful upon the mountains are the feet of him that bringeth good tidings, that publisheth peace; that bringeth good tidings of good, that publisheth salvation:**

that saith unto Zion, thou God reigneth" (Isaiah 62:7). How beautiful would the feet of the missionaries have been to the Hindu couple had they arrived on time to bring them the gospel to save them and their newborn?

The church thrives and makes a greater impact when it is taking the gospel to the lost. This call to witness is a major reason why the Lord promised the disciples the Holy Spirit. He said to them, **"But ye shall receive power after the Holy Ghost is come upon you; and ye shall be witnesses unto me both in Jerusalem, and all Judea, and in Samaria and unto the uttermost parts of the earth" (Acts 1:8).**

The church is empowered to carry out the Great Commission of reaching the ends of the earth with the gospel of Jesus Christ. When the church is faithfully winning souls for the kingdom, revival will be ignited and will also be sustained. It must be noted, however, that the command to reach the world with the good news does not exempt anyone. It is a command given to the leadership and the congregation alike. The argument that "shepherds do not bear sheep, but sheep bear sheep" is absolutely unscriptural and does not stand the test of the Great Commission. It has been the excuse of so many pastors and church leaders who do not know how to, or may be fearful when it come to souls winning. The gospel will only reach the dying world if the church carries out this mandate of Christ with a great sense of urgency.

F)   The Believers' Identity In Christ

One of the most important elements missing from the church today is the believers understanding of their spiritual identity. The spiritual identity answers the question **"Who are you in Christ?"** Knowing who one is in Christ allows him or her to operate with confidence in the tasks assigned by the Lord. One cannot operate or function as a police officer if he or she is not a real Police officer or does not have the credentials to operate in that capacity. It is necessary for the believer to know his or her stand in the Lord and to know the spiritual benefits available unto him or her through Christ. This will strengthen the believer's faith in revival times and enhance his or her relationship with the Lord. The following are just a few of the scriptural verses that point to the believer's identity in Christ:

1) The believer is a child of god.

"As many as received him, to them gave the authority to become the children of God, even to those that believed on his name" (John 1:12).

2) The believer is a new person.

"Therefore if any man be in Christ, he is a new creature; old things are passed away; behold all things are become new" (II Corinthians 5:17).

3) The believer is free from condemnation and is under the spirit of Christ.

"There is therefore now no condemnation to them which are in Christ Jesus, who walk not after the flesh but after the spirit. For the law of the spirit of life in Christ Jesus hath made me free from the law of sin and death" (Romans 8:1&2).

4) The believer is valuable to God.

" For as much as ye know that ye were not redeemed with corruptible things such as silver and gold from your vain conversations received by traditions from your fathers, but with the precious blood of Christ…." (I Peter 1:18&19).

5) The believer is capable of great things for the Lord.

"I can do all things through Christ which strengtheneth me" (Philippians 4:13).

6) The believer's sufficiency is in Christ.

"But my God shall supply all your needs according to his riches by Christ Jesus" (Philippians 4:19).

7) The believer is under divine protection.

"Yea though I walk through the valley of the shadow of death, I will fear no evil; for thou art with me; thy rod and thy staff they comfort" (Psalm 23:4).

8) The Lord's presence is always with the believer.

"Lo, I am with you always even unto the end of the

world" (Matthew 28:20).

9) The believer is trustworthy to the Lord that he has commissioned him or her to be His witness.

"Go ye into all the world, and preach the gospel to every creature." (Mark 16:15).

It is important that the believer knows who he or she is in revival times. This will bolster the confidence of the believer as he or she faces the world and its satanic influences that are bent on coming against the onward march of the church. Knowing the presence and the power of God that is in the believer gives him or her the confident assurance to face the challenges the enemy beings his or her way.

Chapter Six

Readiness To Battle The Enemy

Now when the adversaries… heard that the children of the captivity builded the temple unto the Lord God, then they came unto Zerubbabel and to the chief of the fathers, and said, let us build with you, for we seek your God as you do and we do sacrifice unto him since the days of Esarhaddon king of Assur, which brought us up hither. (Ezra 4:1&2)

Zerubbabel and the elders brought the returning Jews to a place of intimate and closer relationship with their God. They had rebuilt the broken altar of the Lord and offered burnt offerings to Him. The appointed feasts that had been neglected over many generations had now been re-instituted. They had been stirred by the Spirit of God, to give to the rebuilding of the temple.

The work on the temple was under way. Everything seemed

to be going quite well and according to plan. However, Zerubbabel, as a wise revival leader, was alert and ready for whatever the enemy would bring upon them. He had mobilized the children of Israel in battle readiness to defend their faith. Zerubbabel knew who his enemy was, He was alert to the enemy's strategies and battle plans as well as his weapons. Such insightfulness was necessary for the effective mobilization of the people of God for battle.

Whenever the people of God are on the move to do as the Lord has commanded the enemy positions himself to resist. The adage *"never let down your guard"* is very important when you are in the midst of spiritual awakening. Moses learned this when Amalek suddenly attacked then at Rephidim **(See Exodus, 17:8).** The revival leader must be able to identify who the enemy is in order to design an appropriate battle plan against that hindering spirit. The principle to be considered is that one must know the "What" in order to determine the "How." Knowing what kind of enemy one faces will determine how to employ resources according to God's battle plan for defeating the enemy.

Knowing The Enemy

Zerubbabel was a wise revival leader, with great insight into Israel's enemies, the surrounding nations. In fact his awareness of the enemy was a factor in his prompt action to rebuild the altar of the Lord and begin the sacrifices. The altar was a place of meeting with their God and renewing their strength to face challenges head on. The Scripture states, **"And they set the altar upon its bases; for fear was upon them because of the peoples of those countries..." (Ezra, 3:3).** Again the Scripture declares,

"...when the adversaries of Judah and Benjamin heard that the children of the captivity builded the temple unto the Lord God of Israel: Then the people of the land weakened their hands of the people of Judah, and troubled them in building" (Ezra 4:1&4).

Zerubbabel was in a position to interrupt the plans of the enemy because he knew who they were and what they were capable of. Similarly, the modern military undertakes surveillance of the enemy before striking. Indeed Joshua as a great military leader, sent men to spy on the land of Jericho before moving in to attack **(See Joshua 2:1).** By so doing, Joshua was able to assess their strength and any potential challenge they could pose.

As a body of Christ we must know that we have a real enemy who is bent on thwarting all our efforts if possible. Queen Esther knew that Haman, the Agagite, was the enemy of the Jews **(See Esther 3:10).** King Jehoshaphat knew who the enemies of Judah were **(See II Chronicles 20:1&2).** To the young shepherd boy, David, the enemy was an uncircumcised Philistine **(See I Samuel 17:26).** Apostle Paul, identified the enemy the body of Christ is going against this way, "...**principalities, against powers, against the rulers of the darkness of this world, against the spiritual wickedness in the high places." (Ephesians 6:12).**

Paul also identified the kind of armor that the believer must use to defeat this kind of enemy. Paul was in a sense telling the church that once we know the "what," we will be able to determine the "how." That is, if the revival leader and the church can identify the enemy, victory would be assured. The other church, the other brother or sister is not the enemy of the people of God; Satan is. In all the above mentioned cases, the people won a great victory because they had a clear knowledge of who the enemy was. It is quite clear who our enemy is: with Jesus as our captain, we shall know no defeat. The church of Jesus Christ is destined to win as we put our faith in Him.

The Enemy's Tactics

Knowing the enemy also means having insight into his tactics. One of the first tactics the enemy attempted to use against Zerubbabel and the Jews was deception. The enemy tried to use deception to infiltrate and cause confusion among them. The enemy approached Zerubbabel and the elders of the Jews saying, **"...Let us build with you for we seek your God as you do, and we do sacrifice unto him..." (Ezra 4:2).** They were not of the household of God but were determined to deceive them into thinking so. However, Zerubbabel and the Jewish elders quickly recognized this. It was the enemy's plan to infiltrate them with a mixed multitude to turn them against God **(See Numbers, 11:4-6).**

Paul, the apostle warned the Corinthian church of such deceptive tactics of the enemy when he wrote, **"But I fear lest by any means, as the serpent beguiled Eve through his subtlety, so your mind should be corrupted from the simplicity that is in Christ" (II Corinthians, 11:3).** Paul is reminding his audience of the satanic tactics of deception that led to the fall of man in the Garden of Eden. Again Paul declared, **"For were false apostles, deceitful workers, transforming themselves into the apostles of Christ. And no marvel, for Satan himself is transformed into an angel of light. Therefore it is no great thing if his ministers also be transformed into ministers of righteousness, whose end shall be according to their works"(II Corinthians 11:13-15).**

The revival leader and the church must be knowledgeable of the word of God if they are to discern the enemy's deceptive tactics. These are his tactics of old, and he continues to apply the same ones. Unfortunately, many are taken in by it because they are unable to distinguish between "thus says the Lord" and the voice of the enemy.

Another tactic of the enemy is to influence the believer to apply human advice to accomplish a divine assignment. All advice from every man must be verified through prayer and in God's word, with no exception. This is necessary in spite of who the advisor might be.

Moses encountered such a challenge when he took advice

from his father-in-law, Jethro without consulting the Lord. God had called Moses and equipped him to lead the Israelites from Egyptian bondage into the Promised Land. However, when his father-in-law arrived and noticed that the leadership style given Moses by God was unlike what he knew from his country, he inserted himself. He advised Moses to appoint 70 elders to help with the day-to-day running of the congregation **(See Exodus 18:13-26).** This advice sounded spiritual and wise, but it was not what the Lord wanted for Moses and the people at the time. Serious problems followed, because the 70 elders had neither been approved by nor commissioned by the Lord.

His respect for man, almost made Moses lose his focus. He and the Israelites were to follow the pillar of cloud by day and the pillar of fire by night whenever it moved. This was the commandment of the Lord for their wilderness journey **(See Numbers 9:15-23).** However, the influence of Jethro, Moses' father-in-law lingered over him and impaired his spiritual judgment.

When the cloud lifted for the children of Israel to continue their journey, Moses turned to his brother-in-law, Jethro's son to go with them and lead them in their journey rather than following the cloud. Pleading with his brother-in-law to go with them, Moses said, **"Leave us not, I pray thee, forasmuch as thou knowest where we are to encamp in the wilderness, and thou mayest be to us instead of eyes" (Numbers 10:31).** Moses did not just form a leadership team without God's approval, but also took his focus from the pillar of cloud unto a man who was not in a covenant relationship with the God of Israel. This decision on Moses' part opened the floodgate for other challenges in the wilderness journey.

When Moses was on Mount Sinai receiving the Ten Commandments, the people asked Aaron to build them a golden calf to worship instead of the God who had delivered them from bondage **(See Exodus 32:1-6).** Indeed it was the elders appointed by Moses upon the advice of Jethro, his father-in-law that led the people to ask Aaron to build the golden calf. Customary, it was the elders of the people that spoke for them in situations like this.

Later when Moses was not getting much help from the 70 appointed upon Jethro's advice, he said to the Lord, **"I am not able to bear all these people alone, because it is too much" (Numbers, 11:15).** It was at this time that the Lord commanded Moses to select 70 elders, saying, **"...and I will take of the spirit which is upon you, and will put it upon them: and they shall bear the burden of the people with thee, that thou bearest it not thyself alone" (Numbers 11:17).** This set of 70 elders, unlike the ones appointed upon Jethro's advice, was approved by God; and He put the same spirit that was upon Moses upon them **(See Numbers 11:24-29).**

Peter and John seemed to have this incident in mind when they answered the Jewish council and the chief priests thus,

"Whether it be right in the sight of God to hearken unto you more than unto God judge ye" (Acts 4:19). Peter and John took a bold stand to obey God rather them the word of man, in spite of the threats from the Jewish leaders.

Another tactic of the enemy is to discourage revival leaders and the church by belittling them into doubting their gifts, their talents and their strength to resist the forces of darkness. The heathen nations approached Zerubbabel and the elders to join in the rebuilding of the temple of God **(See Ezra 4:2).** This was their way of making themselves indispensable to the Jews; thus making the Jews feel inadequate, and to trust in them rather than using the gifts and talents the Lord had given them. This was totally rejected by Zerubbabel and the elders.

David had a similar experience when he was getting ready to confront Goliath. First his older brother Eliab tried to put him down as a "nobody" with this remark, **"…and with whom have you left those few sheep with in the wilderness?" (I Samuel 17:28).** Eliab was discounting David's marvelous skills as a shepherd who had slain both a bear and lion with his bare hands **(See I Samuel 17:32-37).**

The last thing the revival leader and the church need in the face of a battle is discouragement. David as a wise leader resisted his brother and moved on to seek answers to his questions about Goliath the enemy of Israel. When David finally convinced King Saul to allow him to fight Goliath, Saul offered him the king's armor **(See I Samuel 17:38-40)**. This armor was neither made to David's size nor was he accustomed to it. Even though King Saul made this offer with good intentions, David could have been easily killed by Goliath, had he fought in Saul's armor.

Every "David" must fight his or her Goliath with the armor the Lord has given him or her, and not with someone else's armor. Revival leaders must resist the temptation of copying the visions, the preaching styles and dreams the Lord has given others. Revival leaders must seek the Lord for direction for their particular situations and circumstances. Revival leaders must never allow the enemy to cause them to discount the visions, dreams, abilities and gifts the Lord has given on them.

The Enemy's Battle Plan

The enemy's battle strategies include false pretenses, sudden attacks, consistent harassment, threats and false assimilations with the people of God in order to stir up trouble from within to demoralize them. Out of nowhere, the surrounding nations who had been Israel's adversaries, approached Zerubbabel and the elders of the Jews to offer help in the rebuilding of the temple of God **(Ezra, 4:2)**. This was to get Zerubbabel and the elders off track to infiltrate their ranks and frustrate their efforts. As a visionary leader, Zerubbabel was quick to reject their offer.

Just after crossing the Red Sea, Amalek made a sudden move against Moses and the people of Israel. The Scripture declares,

"Then came Amalek, and fought with Israel at Rephidim." (Exodus 17:8; See also I Samuel 15:2). They ambushed them. The Jews just delivered from the Egyptian bondage were only pyramid builders and had never fought a war, nor did they have any battle experience.

Such sudden attacks by the enemy were aimed at inciting fear and confusion among the people of God and their leaders. These attempts by the enemy came to naught because the Lord intervened on behalf of His people.

Another strategy of the enemy is constant intimidation and harassment. The enemy used this strategy to weaken the efforts of Zerubbabel and the Jews in the rebuilding efforts by troubling them and hiring counselors to file complaint against them with the king of Persia **(See Ezra 4:4&5).**

During the time of Gideon the children of Israel underwent a similar experience from their enemies. They were gripped with fear to the extent that most of them abandoned their homes to live in caves **(See Judges 6:2-6).** However, the God who has promised to be with His people till the end of the age raised up Gideon to defeat the enemies of Israel.

The enemy also uses threats to overpower the revival leader and the people of God. In Zerubbabel's time, the adversaries of the people of God troubled them and even wrote letters to the king to make life miserable **(See Ezra 4:4&5).** It was threats like these that put fear into King Saul and his army. In fact, Saul and the armies of Israel literally ran to hide themselves whenever Goliath, the Philistine giant came out to defile them and to defile the God of Israel.

The Scriptures declare,

"**...there came the champion, the Philistine of Gath, Goliath by name, out of the armies of the Philistines, and spoke according to the same words and David heard them. And all the men of Israel, when they saw the man fled from him, and were sore afraid" (I Samuel 17:23&24; See also I Samuel 17:4-9).** God raised up David at this time to defeat the enemy.

Positioning The Church For Battle In Revival Times

Like a military leader preparing his troops for battle, Zerubbabel, as a revival leader, made sure that the congregation of Israel was not entangled by anything that could hinder their effectiveness on the battle field. One of such potential entanglements was infiltration of the congregation by individuals who may be aligned with the enemy or individuals who do not have the necessary discipline and endurance for spiritual warfare. The revival leader and the church must be discerning of such hindrances.

Zerubbabel as a revival leader, and the elders sensing the enemy's attempt to infiltrate their ranks, quickly recognized and dealt with it without any compromise or hesitation. In responding to the enemy's attempt to infiltrate the body, Zerubbabel and the elders replied, "**…You have nothing to do with us to build a house unto our God; but we ourselves together will build unto the Lord God …**" (**Ezra 4:3**). Zerubbabel was very careful to keep out those who had no covenant relations with the God of Israel. This was to ensure that the people of God were standing fast in one mind and one spirit, striving together for the faith (**see Philippians 1:27**).

During the Exodus from Egypt, mixed multitudes were among the people of God who stirred up a lustful rebellion that turned the wrath of God upon the people in the wilderness. The Scripture declares it this way,

"**And the mixed multitude that were among them fell a lusting; and the children of Israel also wept again and said who shall give us flesh to eat? We remember the fish which we did eat in Egypt freely, the cucumbers, the melons, and the leeks, and the onions and the garlic**" (**Numbers 11:4&5**).

The children of Israel were satisfied with the manna until the mixed multitude complained about it and asked for meat. Instead of looking ahead to the spiritual inheritance the Lord had in store for them, they were looking back to the past to satisfy their lust appetizing desires.

Zerubbabel was not willing to make any compromise nor establish any covenant relationship with their heathen adversaries. This was why he refused to get them involved in the rebuilding of the temple of God. The Lord, during the wilderness journey warned Moses against coming into a covenant relationship with the ungodly nations around them, saying, **"Take heed to thyself lest thou make a covenant with the inhabitants of the land wither thou goest, lest it will be of a snare in the midst of thee" (Exodus 34:12).** Weeding out the corrupt individuals protects the people of God from falling into the enemy's traps.

There is also the need to weed out sin from among the congregation if the revival leader and the people of God are to position themselves for victory over the forces of darkness. Ezra, the scribe, upon arriving at Jerusalem, was quick in separating the people of God from the heathen nations around them.

Ezra ordered the priests and the Levites who had taken wives from among the heathen to divorce them. He was very committed to preserving the messianic line for the coming of the messiah **(See Ezra 9).** For the revival leader and the people of God to experience sustained revival, and be able to defend the faith, there is an urgent need to separate from the ungodly and walk in obedience on the path the Lord has set forth for them.

The Weapons At The Believers' Disposal

The people of God have so many weapons at their disposal to assure them of victory anywhere and at any time against any foe. Zerubbabel's weapon was his ability to stand his ground and his uncommon quality of determination to see God's work through, even in the face of incredible foes. He stood his ground against the heathen nations when they offered to help in the rebuilding of the Lord's temple **(See Ezra 4:1-3)**. He had unique weapons that carried him through the most difficult times. These weapons were not carnal; rather they were mighty in God. Apostle Paul put it this way, **"For though we walk in the flesh, we do not war after the flesh. For the weapons of our warfare are not carnal, but mighty through God to the pulling down of strongholds" (II Corinthians 10:3&5).**

In the case of Nehemiah, the weapon was their great alertness and the ability to multi-task. The Scripture describes it this way," **…every one with one of his hands wrought in the work and with the other hand held a weapon. For the builders everyone had his sword girded by his side and so builded…" (Nehemiah 4:17&18).**

Faith was also a powerful weapon used by Zerubbabel. He and the elders believed strongly in the prophecies concerning the returning of the Jews to their ancestral home and the rebuilding of the city and the temple. This kept him believing even when everything that could be seen with the eye proved contrary **(See Jeremiah 25:11&12; Isaiah 44:28; Isaiah 45:13).** This is very significant because knowing the word, which is the truth does not only enhance ones faith but also affords the believer the central piece of the armor (the belt of truth) that holds the rest of the armor together **(See Romans, 10:17; Ephesians, 6:14).**

However, it must be noted that the Lord can equip the believer with weapons that are strange and do not appeal to the wisdom of conventional warfare; yet they are effective and get the work done. These weapons may look foolish in the eyes of men but God is able to use them for his glory. Apostle Paul put it this way, **"But God hath chosen the foolish things of the world to confound the wise, and God hath chosen the weak things of the world to confound the things which are mighty"** **(I Corinthians 1:27).**

David defeated the Philistine champion, Goliath with a sling and a stone **(See I Samuel 17:40-51).** Even Goliath himself was surprised at it, and remarked, **"Am I a dog that thou comest to me with staves? And the Philistine cursed David by his gods"** **(I Samuel 17:43).**

In the case of Gideon, He defeated combined enemy forces with only 300 men, with broken pitchers, holding lamps and blowing trumpets. The enemies turned on each other till they had destroyed themselves **(See Judges 7:20-23).**

Joshua and the Jews brought down the walls of Jericho without any machinery or bombs. Joshua and the Jews marched around the walls once a day but on the seventh day marched around it seven times. At the end of the march the priests blew their trumpets and with a great shout from the people the walls came tumbling down **(See Joshua 6:13-20).**

King Jehoshaphat mobilized a choir to go before the army to

sing praises to the Lord. The enemies responded by attacking each other and thereby handing victory into the hands of the people of God **(See II Chronicles, 20:21-24).** As foolish as the aforementioned examples may appear, they won victories over their enemies by simply following the instructions of the Lord.

The Lord is able indeed to use foolish things to confound the wise and weak things to confound the mighty. The revival leader must be willing to use the weapons and tools the Lord has placed at his or her disposal with all diligence in order for the victory to be won.

The revival leader must exercise unwavering faith and trust in the God who has ordained him to lead his people. This kind of faith can even turn the jaw bone of an ass into a weapon of mass destruction **(See Judges, 15:15).** This kind of faith is patient and does not question God's directives. Doubt questions but faith complies. Doubt sees the hurdles but faith mounts up with wings of eagle to fly over them. Doubt sees the mountains but faith commands them and they are removed. It is this kind of faith that enables the revival leader and the people of God to attain victory with whatever tools the Lord makes available to them.

Chapter 7

The Waiting Period

Then the people of the land weakened the hands of the people of Judah, and troubled them in building... Then ceased the work on the house of God which is at Jerusalem. So it ceased unto the second year of the reign of Darius, king of Persia. (Ezra 4:4&24)

Zerubbabel and the elders together with the returning Jews had completed the altar and re-instituted the appointed feasts and sacrifices of the Lord. The foundation of the house of the Lord had been laid and the building project was in progress. They were on a spiritual high as everything appeared to be going smoothly for them. Their progress suddenly attracted the enemy's fiercest attacks in an attempt to stop the work on the house of the Lord. Just as they were feeling good about the work the enemy lifted up its ugly head to impede their progress.

The Delaying Tactics Of The Enemy

With each progress of the people of God in revival times comes the enemy's ferocious attacks. Such attacks are aimed at discouraging the people of God into discarding their dreams and vision. The Scripture in a very clear manner described the enemy's efforts to delay the work on the house of the Lord this way,

"Then the people of the land weakened the hands of the people of Judah and troubled them in building. And hired counselors to frustrate their purpose all the days of Cyrus, king of Persia until the days of Darius, king of Persia" (Ezra 4:4). From the time of Cyrus' decree until the reign of Darius when permission was granted to continue with the rebuilding of tem temple was a span of about 15 years. That meant the enemies of the people of God were able to delay progress on the rebuilding of the temple for over 15 years.

The Scripture states, **"Then ceased the work of the house of God which is at Jerusalem. So it ceased unto the second year of the reign of Darius king of Persia" (Ezra 4:24).** This was enough to discourage the people and kill their enthusiasm. As the Lord declared, **" The thief cometh not but for to steal, and to kill, and to destroy…."(John 10:10).** They were highly motivated in their efforts and were hoping to see the temple completed within a set time frame then suddenly the enemy attacked.

The younger generation who never saw the temple of Solomon had shouted a great shout of praise at the completion of the foundation for the temple **(See Ezra 3:11)**. They were anticipating to see a Jewish temple for the first time in their lives. Their hopes had suddenly been dashed. The enemy has been able to use their past against them, by referring to Jerusalem as a rebellious and bad city **(Ezra 4:12)**.

In fact there had been three rebellions with the last one incurring the wrath of Nebuchadnezzar who took them into captivity in Babylon. While our past successes can enslave us into complacency, so our past mistakes and shortcomings can hold us back in the tombstones of past failures. The enemy has the tendency to use our past to bring accusations against us to incite guilt and shame. Indeed the past rebellions were discovered in the Persian archives. This resulted in the king giving a command to halt the work.

The scriptural account on the king's response in a letter to the governor of the province states, **" Give ye now commandment to cause these men to cease, and that this city be not built, until another commandment be given from me"** (Ezra 4:1).

Discouragement followed, resulting in the neglect of the work of the Lord. The people turned to their own things **(See Haggai 1:1-4)**. Through the prophet Haggai, the Lord spoke to the people to go back to the building project saying, **"Go up to the mountains and bring wood, and build the house; and I will take pleasure in it, and I will be glorified, saith the Lord"** **(Haggai 1:8)**. They had succumbed to the pressures of the enemy.

This was when even the strongest revival leaders could begin to question their own calling.

When you feel you are hearing from God, and speaking those things into the lives of the congregation, and yet nothing is happening or they are not being received, discouragement and frustration can set in. Zerubbabel and Jeshua the high priest were discouraged. The leaders were under such satanic attacks that the Lord had to intervene to bring about their vindication **(Zechariah 3:1-7)**.

The Lord does not abandon His own when discouragement sets in. He has promised, **"...lo I am with you always, even unto the end of the earth" (Matthew 28:20).** The Psalmist gave even a stronger assurance from the Lord when he wrote, **"Yea though I walk through the valley of the shadow of death, I will fear no evil, for thou art with me, thy rod and thy staff they comfort me" (Psalm 23:4).** Often when leaders are experiencing unfulfilled dreams and visions, discouragement sets in for them to feel all alone like everyone has abandoned them. Many have given up under such circumstances.

The God who has called you to do his will is much closer than you can ever imagine. Zerubbabel realized he was not alone and that all was not lost, when Zechariah prophesied specifically to his leadership and the Lord's favor on his life and ministry, saying, **"The hands of Zerubbabel have laid the foundation of this house; his hands shall also finish it, and thou shall know** that the Lord of hosts hath sent me unto you" (Zechariah 4:9). The revival leader must understand that delays are bound to occur but the Lord is always there to see his people through those tough times.

Turning Delays Into Waiting

Delays are a normal part of life. However, when it is experienced in the midst of revival it could perpetuate intense frustrations and discouragement on the part of the revival leadership and the congregation. The work they were doing had suddenly stopped because of the enemy's attacks **(Ezra 4:24)**. The way the revival leader and the people of God handle delays will determine whether they become blessings or defeat.

The delay experienced by Zerubbabel and the returning Jews temporary turned into a defeat. The people turned away from the work on the house of the Lord to focus on their own homes and businesses. Because of the enemy's attacks the work of the Lord had ceased to be a priority and become a secondary matter. They had stopped the work on the house of the Lord with the hope that it would make the enemy go away.

This was a wrong strategy. The Lord therefore spoke against this neglect on the part of the people through prophet Haggai saying, **"…This people say the time is not come, the time that the Lord's house should be built. It is time for you, O ye to dwell in ceiled houses and this house lie in waste?" (Haggai 1:2-4).**

The enemy's attacks were making them conclude that the time was not ripe for the Lord's house to be built. The Lord through prophet Haggai said that in spite of the enemy's attacks the work must continue because it was the right time. Satanic attacks do not imply that we are out of the Lord's will. If anything, the enemy attacks when the people of God are on the right track for the things of God.

In truth, a delay in the midst of doing the will of the Lord must be turned into a period of waiting and seeking the Lord for direction. Such waiting breeds strength and vigor for the work in which the Lords has called us. Prophet Isaiah put it this way, **"But they that wait upon the Lord shall renew their strength; they shall mount with wings as eagles; they shall run and not be weary; they shall walk and not faint" (Isaiah 40:31).**

The period of waiting is not an easy task. This is probably why many pastors and church leaders rush into things, rather than waiting on the Lord for divine instructions. Often times, because leaders are not waiting on the Lord, they make plans and expect the Lord to put his stamp of approval upon them. This could destroy a ministry and cause serious damage to the people of God. In spite of the pain involved, it pays to wait on the Lord for his timing and leading.

Let's consider the life of an eagle as it renews itself. Those who have lived in the countryside or the rural areas and have some experience with the behavior of eagles understand what the

Psalmist meant when he wrote, **"Who satisfieth thy mouth with good things, so that they youth is renewed like the eagle's" (Psalm 103:5).**

An old eagle finds it difficult to fly swiftly to the prey like the younger ones. This could cause the old eagle to starve even unto death. To survive, the old eagle will therefore fly to a high mountain and seek out a place of safety near a source of a stream where there are neither insects nor any predators to harm it. There it will pluck off all its wings and feathers and dip itself in the water. This causes the eagle great pain. At the same time the eagle becomes vulnerable because it could neither fly nor defend itself. The eagle is at this time hungry. It patiently waits and spends most of its time sharpening its beak on the rock to make it as sharp as that of a young eagle. Over time the eagle will grow new wings and feathers, and its beak will be very sharp as it was when it was young. This process is long and arduous, yet the eagle is willing to put itself through it in order to renew its youth and fly to seek out the prey, like any other young eagle on the block.

For a revival leader to mount up with wings like the eagle's he must be prepared to wait on the Lord till he hears His voice or knows His perfect will in whatever circumstance he finds himself. If the revival leader is able to turn delays into waiting on the Lord, he will know no defeat. He will be renewed with strength and vigor to be victorious in the Lord.

Habakkuk, the prophet, encouraged the people of God not

to give up on waiting on the Lord when the vision or the prophetic word given is delayed this way, **" For the vision is yet for an appointment time, but at the end it will speak, and not lie: though it tarry wait for it; because it will surely come, it will not tarry" (Habakkuk 2:3)**. A delayed vision or prophetic word from the Lord does not mean it will not be fulfilled.

We serve a God who keeps his promises as we patiently wait on him. The disciples were admonished by the Lord to wait and not depart from Jerusalem for the father's promise of the Holy Spirit **(Acts 1:4&5; See also Isaiah 54:3; Psalm 27:14; Psalm 37:7&34; Psalm 130:6).**

Delays should not be allowed to become defeats. They must be turned into moments of blessings by seeing them as signals to continue waiting on the Lord until divine directions are made clear unto us. Daniel set himself to intercede for his people Israel and encountered some delays due to the enemy's opposition in the spirit realm. He never gave up. He remained steadfast in waiting on the Lord until he got the breakthrough.

The Scripture declares his breakthrough this way, **"And behold a hand touched me which set me upon my knees, and upon the palms of my hands...Then said he unto me, fear not Daniel for from the first day thou set thine heart to understand, and to chasten thyself before thy God thy words were heard, and I am come for thy words, but the prince of the kingdom of Persia withstood me for one and twenty days;**

but lo, Michael, one of the chief princes came to help me; and I remained there with the kings of Persia. Now I am come to make thee understand what shall befall thy people in the latter days; for the vision is yet for many days" (Daniel 10:11-14).** Daniel could have easily missed a divine appointment had he allowed the delay to become a defeat and had he given up. The author of the book of Hebrews encouraging the people of God to persevere in seeking Him wrote, **"Cast not away therefore your confidence which hath great recompense of reward. For ye have need of patience, that, after ye have done the will of God, ye shall revive the promise" (Hebrews 10:33).** Though waiting could be painful and challenging, it is never in vain.

The Voice Of God In The Midst Of Delays

Delays in ministry do not mean the Lord has forgotten his own. God is always at work on behalf of His people even if everything the eyes see indicates otherwise. Zerubbabel was in the midst of a delay of ministry. Most of the people had given up to focus on their own things. As a revival leader, Zerubbabel waited on the Lord, rather than allowing the delays to become a defeat. He finally heard the Lord as he waited. The word of God declares, **"Then the prophets, Haggai the prophet, and Zechariah the son of Iddo, prophesied unto the Jews that were in Judah and in Jerusalem in the name of the God of Israel even unto them" (Ezra 5:1).** These prophetic voices had messages for the revival leadership and the people of God to quicken them for the task ahead.

The prophet Haggai challenged the people to pay attention to the Lord's work rather than their own things **(See Haggai 1:20).** The Lord again spoke through Haggai saying, **"Yet now be strong O Zerubbabel, saith the Lord; and be strong O Joshua, son of Josedech, the high priest; and be strong all ye people of the land, saith the Lord, and work; for I am with you saith the Lord of hosts. According to the word that I covenanted with you when you came out of Egypt, so my spirit remaineth among you; fear not" (Haggai 1:4&5).** The Lord encouraged them to continue the work on the house of the Lord because He is with them even in the midst of all the enemy's attacks.

Then came the prophecies of Zechariah, which happened just after Haggai's and stirred them again to pay attention to the Lord's work. The prophet was awakened by the angel of the Lord, who asked him,

"What do you see? And I said I have looked, and behold a candlestick all of gold, with a bowl upon the top of it, and has seven lamps thereon, and seven pipes to the seven lamps, which are upon the top thereof; and two olive trees by it, one upon the right side of the bowl and the other upon the left side thereof …Then he answered and spake unto me saying, This is the word of the Lord unto Zerubbabel, saying Not by might, not by power, but by my spirit, saith the Lord of hosts" (Zechariah 4:4-6).

Zechariah's prophecy reminded Zerubbabel and reminded

the elders of God's provisions for the task. He was reminding them of the anointing that is available to the people of God to accomplish divine tasks. This was depicted by the olive trees and the oil that is coming through the pipes into the lamps.

The Lord also reminded Zerubbabel that it is not by might or how much he stretches himself that would get the work done. Neither could he get the work done by his power, by his position in the society nor by his intellectual abilities. The Lord through this prophet is saying to Zerubbabel and all revival leaders that the work assigned us by the Lord could only be accomplished through the anointing He bestows upon us. This is very important because leaders and the people of God have the tendency to force things rather than relying solely on the Lord. The Lord has not called us to make things happen but rather to allow Him to do His will through us and with us.

The Lord further encouraged Zerubbabel with a word from Prophet Zechariah saying, **"The hands of Zerubbabel have laid the foundation of this house, his hands shall also finish it, and thou shalt know that the Lord of host has sent me unto you" (Zechariah 4:9).** This word lifted Zerubbabel out of discouragement into action. He was reminded of the Lord, that just as He used him to lay the foundation of the temple so will He use him to finish it.

Zerubbabel and the elders heard the word of the Lord that the delay does not mean the work has stopped. The voice of the

Lord, in the midst of our delays in ministry, puts something inside of the believer that tells him or her to go on. It removes all the fears and the doubts and puts within the believer the faith and courage to do the work the Lord has called him or her into.

The Stirring Of The Spirit Of The Revival Leader

When the Lord speaks, His words do not return empty. Affirming His faithfulness in fulfilling His word, the Lord spoke through prophet Isaiah, saying, **"So shall my word be that goeth forth out of my mouth; it shall not return unto me void, but it shall accomplish that which I please and it shall prosper in the things whereto I sent it" (Isaiah 55:11).** God's word was indeed accomplished as Zerubbabel and the elders, together with the people, mobilized themselves to work on the house of the Lord.

"And the Lord stirred up the spirit of Zerubbabel the son of Shealtiel, governor of Judah, and the spirit of Joshua the son of Josedech, the high priest, and the spirit of all the remnant of the people, and they came and did work in the house of the Lord of hosts, their God" (Haggai 1:14; See also Ezra 5:1-5).

As revival leaders and the people of God wait on the Lord they shall indeed renew their strength and vigor to carry out the assignments the Lord has called them to undertake. The voice of the Lord has removed the clouds of frustrations, discouragement, and doubt and ushered them into a new arena of faith and commitment to the heavenly call.

Divine Favor

We serve a God who is able to turn the king's heart in our favor. King Solomon declared, **"The king's heart is in the hands of the Lord, as the rivers of water; he turneth it whithersoever he will" (Proverbs 21:1).** When the Lord spoke through the prophets to Zerubbabel, he was at the same time working on the heart of the king of Persia to grant them favor. Our God, who is the Kings of kings and the Lord of lords, is able to use any ruler of this world to accomplish his purpose on behalf of his people **(See Isaiah 44:28; Isaiah 45:1&13; Ezra 1:2).**

Zerubbabel as a revival leader has received the prophetic word and placed his faith, trust and confidence in the Lord who had spoken to him. As he stepped out by faith to do the Lord's will, divine favor followed him all the way. When the enemies appealed to the king to search the records it was found that a decree had indeed been made to allow and support them in the rebuilding of the house of the Lord **(See Ezra 6:1-5).**

When the decree of Cyrus was found, King Darius told the peoples of the nations to leave the Jews alone to rebuild the temple of their God. The king did not only agree with Cyrus' decree but went even further with a very strong decree stating,

"Moreover I make a decree what ye shall do to the elders of these Jews for the building of this house of God: that of the king's goods, *even* of the tribute beyond the river, forthwith expenses be given unto these men, that they be not hindered.

And that which they have need of, both young bullocks, and rams, and lambs, for the burnt offerings of the God of heaven, wheat, salt, wine, and oil, according to the appointment of the priests which are at Jerusalem, let it be given them day by day without fail: That they may offer sacrifices of sweet savours unto the God of heaven, and pray for the life of the king, and of his sons. Also I have made a decree, that whosoever shall alter this word, let timber be pulled down from his house, and being set up, let him be hanged thereon; and let his house be made a dunghill for this. And the God that hath caused his name to dwell there destroy all kings and people that shall put to their hand to alter and to destroy this house of God which is at Jerusalem. I, Darius, have made a decree; let it be done with speed" (Ezra 6:8-12).

King Darius' decree strengthened the hands of Zerubbabel and the returning Jews in the rebuilding of the house of the Lord, with all expenses paid in full. All the provisions needed for sacrifices were made available to them by the king's command. Because of the Lord's favor, the people who lacked were now overflowing with abundance.

The hand of the Lord was so strong on the king that he specified severe punishment of anyone who would alter the decree to hinder the efforts of Zerubbabel and the returning Jews. Indeed, what the enemy meant for evil, God is able to turn around for the good of His people **(See Genesis 50:20).** The children of Israel finally completed the house of the Lord.

The Scripture declares,

"And the elders of the Jews builded and they prospered through the prophesying of Haggai, the prophet and Zechariah, the son of Iddo. And they builded, and finished it, according to the commandment of the God of Israel, and according to the commandment of Cyrus, and Darius and Artaxerxes, Kings of Persia. And the house was finished on the third of the month Adar which was in the sixth year of the reign of Darius the king" (Ezra 6:14-15).

The blessings and the favor of the Lord, as prophesied by Isaiah, the prophet, are fulfilled **(See Isaiah 44:28; Isaiah 45:13)**. For the first time in over 70 years the Jews were able to celebrate the Passover **(See Ezra 6:19-22)**. A reminder of the mighty deliverance by their God from the Egyptian bondage **(Exodus 12:13&14)**.

The Lord also affirmed His seal of approval upon the new temple. The priests, the Levites and the fathers who were elderly and saw the temple of Solomon wept when the foundation was laid **(Ezra 3:12)**. The Lord defused their fears and doubts, saying,

"...I will fill this house with my glory saith the Lord... The glory of this latter house shall be greater than of the former, saith the Lord of hosts; and in this place will I give peace, saith the Lord of hosts" (Haggai 2:7&9). Zerubbabel had turned delay into waiting on his God. He was greatly rewarded with overwhelming favor from the Lord. The house of the Lord was now completed and accepted by the Lord with His promise of great glory being upon it.

Zerubbabel did not give up. He stood firm in faith when everything around him spoke to the contrary. In the midst of delays, the revival leader must hold fast to the promises the Lord has made to him.

For He who has called us to do His work is the One who initiated that work in us. Apostle Paul put it this way, **"Being confident of this very thing, that he which hath began a good work in you will perform it until the day of Jesus Christ" (Philippians 1:6).** The God who has called us is able to complete what He has started in us. This word is a blessing for every revival leader to hold fast to. Therefore, we cannot lose heart. Even in the face of the greatest adversity, the revival leader must remember that the Lord who has started His work in him, through him and with him will complete what He started.

Chapter 8

The Anointing Oil

And thou shall make it an oil of holy ointment, an ointment compound after the art of the apothecary; it shall be a holy anointing oil...Whosoever compoundeth any like it shall be cut off from the people. **(Exodus 30:25&33)**

In the most difficult moment of Zerubbabel's ministry, the Lord through prophet Zechariah, reminded him that it is not by how much he stretches himself or by his status among the people, but by the Spirit of God **(Zechariah 4:6).** This was depicted by the oil of anointing that flowed out of the two olive trees into the lamps. This is how the prophet described the vision,

"Now the angel who talked with me came back and wakened me, as a man who is wakened out of his sleep. And he said to me, 'What do you see?' So I said, 'I am looking, and there *is* a lamp stand of solid gold with a bowl on top of it, and on the stand seven lamps with seven pipes to the seven lamps. Two olive trees are by it, one at the right of the bowl and the other at its left.' So I answered and spoke to the angel who talked with me, saying, 'What are these, my lord?' Then the angel who talked with me answered and said to me, 'Do you not know what these are?' And I said, 'No, my lord.' So he answered and said to me: 'This is the word of the LORD to Zerubbabel: 'Not by might nor by power, but by My Spirit,' Says the LORD of hosts" (Zechariah 4:1-6).

The anointing of God is necessary if a revival leader or any leader of God's people is to be able to accomplish that which the Lord has assigned them.

Zerubbabel had followed the law and adhered to the prophecies concerning the return of the Jews to their ancestral home and the rebuilding of the temple, yet he experienced a roadblock along the way. This caused a delay of over 15 years. Zerubbabel had done all he could, yet the work on the house of the Lord had come to a standstill. It was at this time that the Lord spoke to him in a vision through Zechariah, the prophet regarding the oil of anointing.

The continuity of the flow of oil from the olive trees into the lamps is an indication that El Shaddai, the Lord who is enough has an unlimited supply of oil to anoint His people and to keep the church ablaze for Christ. Like Zerubbabel, all God's people need His anointing to accomplish the tasks assigned them. The importance of the anointing was echoed by Jesus, the son of God, at the beginning of his earthly ministry.

When Jesus went to the synagogue in Nazareth, his hometown, he was handed the book of the prophet Isaiah, and he turned to the passage that affirmed his Messiaship saying, '**The Spirit of the LORD is upon Me, because he hath anointed me to preach the gospel to the poor, he hath sent me to heal the brokenhearted; to preach deliverance to the captives, and recovering of sight to the blind, to set at liberty them that are bruised; to preach the acceptable year of the LORD"** (Luke 4:18 & 19; See also Isaiah 61:1 & 2).

In its simplest terms, anointing is an empowerment from God upon his called out ones to carry out his ordained purposes. The ancient Kings of Israel, the priests and the prophets were anointed because they had been set apart by God to carry out specific tasks among his people **(See Psalm 133:2; I Samuel 10:1; I Samuel 16:12&13).**

However, the word "anointing" is so often overused and misused among Christians, especially within some charismatic circles. The term is often erroneously ascribed to a preacher when he or she is loud or shouting from the pulpit. Many even perceive being emotional in the church or in the pulpit as being under the anointing. Others see the opposite as being under the anointing. While some of these preachers may be under the anointing, that is not necessarily the Biblical standard of the anointing. This chapter will attempt to shed some light on what anointing truly is by looking at the characteristics of the ingredients that were used to compound the anointing oil.

Ingredients Of The Holy Anointing Oil

Immediately after telling Moses how Aaron and the priests should purify themselves before entering the Tabernacle to perform their priestly duties, the Lord gave Moses an instruction on how to compound the anointing oil with very select ingredients in very specific quantities. It is very significant and worth noting that out of the four ingredients, the Lord required the amount of two of them to be 500 shekels each while the other two were to be 250 shekels each.

The Lord spoke to Moses saying, **"...Take thou also unto thee principal spices, of pure myrrh five hundred shekels, and of sweet cinnamon half so much, even two hundred and fifty shekels, and of sweet calamus two hundred and fifty shekel. And of cassia five hundred shekels, after the shekel of the sanctuary, and of olive oil a hin" (Exodus 30:22-24).**

Myrrh (Humility/Enduring Faith)

The Lord told Moses to take 500 shekels of pure myrrh. There are certain characteristics of the myrrh that need to be considered here. When the bark of the tree that produces the myrrh is cut, the liquid myrrh flows out but flows out slowly. When the liquid dries on the bark of the tree it looks like a tear drop. As a result the people of ancient Mesopotamia had considered it to symbolize "humility." Also the myrrh has been used to numb pain. This is symbolic of "endurance."

These characteristics of the myrrh point to the qualities of humility and enduring faith or perseverance. These are very important characteristics that are to be apparent in the life of any man or woman of God who claims to be operating under the anointing. It is important to note that the Myrrh is one of the two principal ingredients that the Lord required 500 shekels of. This indicates that the Lord sees humility and endurance as very important in the lives of the men and women He has called to carry out his mandate.

The humility of Moses, the servant of God is described this way, **"Now the man Moses was very meek, above all the men who were upon the face of the earth" (Numbers 12:3).** Moses' humility was so pleasing to God that those who tried to exploit it for selfish gains were met with divine wrath **(See Numbers 12:1-9).** Pride comes before a fall.

The humility and the enduring faith of Jesus, the anointed

of God is described by Apostle Paul this way,

"Let this mind be in you which was also in Christ Jesus, who, being in the form of God, did not consider it robbery to be equal with God, but made Himself of no reputation, taking the form of a bondservant, and coming in the likeness of men. And being found in appearance as a man, He humbled Himself and became obedient unto death, even the death of the cross" (Philippians 2:5-8). These qualities of humility and enduring faith are greatly rewarded by the Lord. James declared, **"God resisteth the proud but giveth grace to the humble" (James 4:6).**

Humility also places the believer in a position to overcome the devices of the enemy. The Scripture puts it this way, **"Be humble, be vigilant: because your adversary the devil, as a roaring lien, walked about seeking whom he may devour" (I Peter 5:8).**

In addressing the lack of faith of his disciples, Jesus said, **"…If ye have faith as a grain of mustard seed, ye shall say unto this mountain, remove hence to yonder place, and it shall remove: and nothing shall be impossible to you" (Matthew 17:20).** The Lord was not just talking only about the smallness of the mustard seed, but more importantly about the enduring qualities of the seed.

Normally, the tap root of a typical plant avoids big stones and slabs of rocks when growing in order for its roots to grow deep into the soil to extract nutrients. The mustard seed is the contrary. Its tap root does not avoid large stones or slab of racks. The tap root will stay on top of the slab of rock till it gradually penetrates it and makes it a part of its foundation. It does not give up until it breaks through the slab of rock in its path. This makes the growth process of the mustard tree a little slower and unlike other plants. It grows rapidly after breaking through the slabs of rocks in its path. The mustard plant makes the slab of rock a part of its foundation, and thereby, enabling it to be able to withstand heavy storms.

While the other plants around the mustard tree are being uprooted by the heavy winds and storms, the mustard tree stands firm. The faith, like a mustard seed, does not give up on its God-given visions and dreams; it is rather persistent and determined. Like the Scripture says, **"Cast not away therefore your faith (confidence) which has great recompense of reward. For you have need of endurance (patience) that, after ye have done the will of God, ye shall receive the promise"** (Hebrews 10:35&36). Like the mustard seed, the Lord wants his church to hold fast to her faith till the answer or the promise is fulfilled.

My personal experience with many pastors today is that they move from one vision to another when they do not see the expected outcomes as quickly as they want to. They are like a person praying for patience this way, "God give me patience, and by the way I want it right now."

This attitude on the part of some pastors and church leaders has only contributed to creating a new generation of believers with **"microwave mentality"**- that is; whatever they ask of the Lord should come quickly. Many also try to force things to happen by adopting the **Rebekah Principle** which says, "I heard clearly from the Lord, but I need to help the situation because it does not seem to be going the way it should." **(See Genesis 25:22&23; Genesis 26:1-30).**

Endurance is the oil that greases the engine of faith to stay expecting. In emphasizing the importance of faith that endures, Oral Roberts rightly coined the slogan, **"Never give up for your miracle is on the way".**

Cinnamon (Boldness)

The cinnamon tree has a peculiar characteristic that is of great significance in understanding the nature of the anointing. The people of the Ancient Near East had referred to this tree by saying, **"the bold one has come."** When the cinnamon is growing it is believed to spread out its roots under the surrounding trees. As it gets bigger and taller its spread out roots uproot the other trees around it. The surrounding trees may be bigger and taller, yet the roots of the cinnamon tree will still go against them to uproot them. Cinnamon is never threatened by the height or the size of the surrounding trees. It expands her territory by removing the other trees. It has faith in its ability to remove or uproot them.

Hence that expression, **"the bold one has come."**

Boldness requires knowing what one is made of. David the shepherd boy knew what he was made of when he came face-to-face with the Philistine giant. He knew without a shadow of a doubt that the God in him was greater and mightier than the enemy that was coming against him. Apostle John put it this way, **"You are of God little children, and have overcome them; because greater is he that is in you than he that is in the world" (I John 4:4).** He had killed a bear and a lion with his bare hands and knew that the one who helped him to accomplish such great feats was greater than any incredible foe that he faced.

The Scripture declares,

"Then David said to Saul, 'Let no man's heart fail because of him; your servant will go and fight with this Philistine.' And Saul said to David, 'You are not able to go against this Philistine to fight with him; for you *are* a youth, and he a man of war from his youth.' But David said to Saul, 'Your servant used to keep his father's sheep, and when a lion or a bear came and took a lamb out of the flock, I went out after it and struck it, and delivered *the lamb* from its mouth; and when it arose against me, I caught *it* by its beard, and struck and killed it. Your servant has killed both lion and bear; and this uncircumcised Philistine will be like one of

them, seeing he has defied the armies of the living God'" (I Samuel 17:32-36).

In spite of his size and the fact that even King Saul and the armies of Israel were fearful of Goliath, David was not. He trusted in his roots, which were spread out and deeply grounded in the God of Israel to go up and defeat the Philistine champion. This kind of boldness does not operate in a vacuum, but by faith. Apostle Paul put it this way, **"For we walk by faith, but not by sight" (II Corinthians 5:17).**

When boldness is replaced by fear, doubt and discouragement, the revival leader and the people of God will not be able to stand the challenges of ministry. When 10 of the spies sent to check out the Promised Land returned with evil reports, the people were overtaken with fear and ready to rebel against Moses. They had seen the miracles wrought by God at the hands of Moses. They had also seen the great miracle of the parting of the Red Sea, yet fear had suddenly sapped out their faith and replaced it with unbelief. The positive reports of Caleb and Joshua helped minimize the situation but divine wrath was incurred **(See Numbers, 13:26-14:1-12).**

Calamus (Continual Giving)

Calamus is a very unique plant. It is probably the only plant that produces about seven times per year. It is appropriately referred to in the Ancient Near East as **"the tree that gives again**

and again." It is often thought in recent years that church leaders and pastors are only at the receiving end to enrich themselves. Some leaders in the church have indeed amassed wealth at the expense of the church. This behavior of a few bad apples has given the pastoral ministry a bad rap.

The characteristic of this particular ingredient, calamus, denotes the lifestyle of giving of self and substance to God. The calamus tree does not restrict its giving to a particular season. It produces again and again at least seven times per year. This gives a snapshot of the divine attribute of love. Because He loved, God gave. The Lord has no pleasure in that which it of no value or our left over's. He desires our best, big or small. In declaring his distaste of worthless giving the Lord said,

> **"Ye offer polluted bread upon mine altar; and ye say, wherein have we polluted thee? In that ye say, The table of the LORD is contemptible. And if ye offer the blind for sacrifice, is it not evil? And if ye offer the lame and sick, is it not evil? Offer it now unto thy governor; will he be pleased with thee, or accept thy person? Saith the LORD of hosts" (Malachi 1:7 & 8).**

King David in refusing a free gift to offer to the Lord said, "…Grant me the place of this threshing floor, that I may build an altar therein unto the LORD: thou shalt grant it me for the full price: that the plague may be stayed from the people. And

Ornan said unto David, Take it to thee, and let my lord the king do that which is good in his eyes: lo, I give thee the oxen also for burnt offerings, and the threshing instruments for wood, and the wheat for the meat offering; I give it all. And King David said to Ornan, Nay; but I will verily buy it for the full price: for I will not take that which is thine for the LORD, nor offer burnt offerings without cost. "(I Chronicles 21:22-24).

The Scripture states, **"For God so loved the world that he gave his only begotten son…" (John 3:16).** Our God is a giving God. Jesus the Christ (the anointed one) gave it all on the cross saying, **"…But I am come that they might have and that they might have it more abundantly" (John 10:10).** God did not give us his left over. He gave us his only begotten son, the Best of the best. Jesus did not give only 10 percent of himself, but rather he gave his all, 100 percent on the cross for you and me. The Lord is not asking for a tithe of our lives; he is asking for our all in all.

Giving was what the Lord used to test Abraham's faith and obedience to Him **(See Genesis 22:1-18).** Unless leaders and believers let go of what is in their hands unto the Lord, He will not release unto us that which He has in store for us. The question we must answer to ourselves is this, **"If we cannot trust Him with our money or time or talent, how can we honestly say we can trust Him with our whole life?"** Abraham passed the test by trusting the Lord with his best. Isaac his promised son.

The Scripture states the blessings of giving and receiving this way,

"Give and it shall be given unto you good measure, pressed together and shaken together, and running over shall men give unto your bosom. For with the same measure ye mete withal it shall be measured to you again" (Luke 6:38). The scripture again states that, "… **it is more blessed to give than to receive" (Acts 20:35).** The revival leader and the people of God will experience the outpouring of His favor and blessings if we shall give our all in all unto him as living sacrifices **(see Romans 12:1).**

Cassia (Inner Purity)

The cassia is an herb that is used in the Ancient Near East for medicinal purposes to relieve conditions like constipation. It is therefore associated with inner cleansing. Note that the Lord required Moses to take 500 shekels of this spice in the compounding of the anointing oil. This was the Lord's way of communicating the importance of inner purity and holiness to his people. The man or woman called by God to lead His people or carry out His ordained purpose must pursue inner purity. This is a must and is not optional. The Scripture declares that God is holy **(See Isaiah, 5:3; John 17:11).**

In affirming that the holy God demands holiness of those He calls, Apostle Peter wrote, **"But as he which hath called you is holy, so be ye holy in all manner of conversation" (I Peter 1:15; See also Ephesians, 1:4; II Timothy, 1:9).** The call to Christ is a call to holiness. For without holiness, the Scripture declares, no one shall see God **(Hebrews 12:14).** The man or woman called by God must walk in purity and righteousness. The Scripture says, **"thou art of purer eyes than to behold evil…"(Habakkuk 1:13).** The holy God will not look upon the leader or the believer with favor if he or she is not walking in purity or holiness.

It is very important to note that for both myrrh (humility and enduring faith) and cassia (inner purity and holiness) the Lord told Moses to include 500 shekels worth of each in compounding the anointing oil. It does point to the fact that humility and inner purity are very important characteristics that must be evident in the life of the man or woman who claims to be walking in the anointing. Boldness and the giving of self and substance will follow when the revival leadership and the people of God are walking in humility and holiness.

The absence of these two qualities could spell the downfall of a revival leader or pastor. Cases in point are the sudden public spectacle that Jim Bakker and Jimmy Swaggart experienced in the '80s and the '90s. All these ingredients (myrrh, cinnamon, calamus and cassia) are mixed in their specified proportions with olive oil to compound the Holy Anointing Oil.

Unique Use Of The Oil

The Lord specifically instructed Moses to use the oil to anoint all the items in the Tabernacle and also to anoint Aaron and all those that will occupy the priestly office from generation to generation saying,

"**And thou shalt make it an oil of holy ointment, an ointment compound after the art of the apothecary: it shall be a holy anointing oil. And thou shalt anoint the tabernacle of the congregation therewith, and the ark of the testimony, And the table and all his vessels, and the candlestick and his vessels, and the altar of incense, And the altar of burnt offering with all his vessels, and the laver and his foot. And thou shalt sanctify them, that they may be most holy: whatsoever toucheth them shall be holy. And thou shalt anoint Aaron and his sons, and consecrate them, that they may minister unto me in the priest's office" (Exodus 30:25-30).**

The psalmist described the anointing of Aaron this way, **"It is like a precious ointment upon the head, that ran down upon the beard, even Aaron's beard; that went down to the skirts of his garments" (Psalm 133:2).** Thus everything and every person set apart for God's purpose must be anointed: In other words, they must be empowered from on high to be used for God's glory.

There were also some very peculiar uses of oil by shepherds in the days of David. David wrote in relation to that saying,**"Yea, thou I walk through the valley of the shadow of death, I will fear no evil: for thou art with me; thy rod and thy staff they comfort me" (Psalm 23:4).**

It is believed that there were poisonous snakes that hid in

the desert sand in the valleys. These were a great threat to the flock because they were not easily detected. Unlike the wild predators that could be easily seen by the shepherd these snakes could bite the sheep and disappear into their holes in the sand. As a result, shepherds lost sheep to poisonous snake bites every time they walked through the valley.

The shepherd's strategy to prevent snake bites was to walk cautiously through the valley first and pour oil into all the holes where these snakes might be hiding. The oil made the snakes slippery and thereby unable to climb out of their hole and bite. With the staff and the rod in his hands, the shepherd would kill any snake that showed its head before the oil was poured into its hole. It was only after this painstaking exercise that the shepherd would lead his flock through the valley. No wonder, David called it "the valley of the shadow of death."

Oil was also very important to the shepherds as a remedy against flies that tormented their flock. The psalmist wrote, "**… thou anointest my head with oil; my cup runneth over." (Psalm 23:5).** The psalmist was quite familiar with this use of oil by shepherds. In the Spring, there were certain flies which tended to lay their eggs in the nostrils of the sheep. As the eggs hatch, the little flies crawled and fed on the membrane of the sheep's nostrils. The sheep struggled to breath and could hardly pay attention to the shepherd.

In their attempt to relieve themselves of the discomfort, the sheep continued to bang their heads against a tree or a rock. This often proved fatal. To alleviate this problem and restore sanity to the flock, the shepherds mixed sulphur with olive oil and rubbed it on the nose and the hair of the sheep. The scent of the sulphur caused the little flies to come out of the nostrils and relieved the sheep of all the discomfort. As a result the sheep were able to focus and respond to the shepherd's call.

As God's flock, the church needs this oil of anointing today to keep us safe and give us clarity of thought, in order to focus on the leading of the Holy Spirit. Speaking through the prophet about the coming deliverance for Israel from the yoke of their enemies, the Lord said, **"...his burden shall be taken away from off thy shoulder, and his yoke from off thy neck, and the yoke shall be destroyed because of the anointing"** (Isaiah 10:27). The anointing not only empowers the church but also destroys the enemy's plans against her.

Divine Warning

The instructions for the anointing oil did not come to Moses without a warning. The Lord cautioned the children of Israel on the use of the anointing oil in four specific areas saying,

> **"And thou shalt speak unto the children of Israel, saying, this shall be a holy anointing oil unto me throughout your generations. Upon man's flesh**

shall it not be poured, neither shall ye make any other like it, after the composition of it: it is holy, and it shall be holy unto you. Whosoever compoundeth any like it, or whosoever putteth any of it upon a stranger, shall even be cut off from his people"** (Exodus 30:31-33).

The following are the four specific warnings:

1) **Not To Be Overlooked**

The Lord reminded Moses over and over that the oil shall be a holy anointing oil unto Him throughout all the generations. The Lord did not want them to defile it for it was holy and of value unto Him. In fact the Lord's anger was rekindled against His people when the priest and the leaders defiled those things which were holy unto Him.

The Lord stated this in strong terms through the prophet Ezekiel saying, **"Her priests have violated my law, and have profaned my holy things: they have put no difference between the holy and profane, neither have they showed difference between the unclean and the clean…"** (Ezekiel 22:26). The Lord wants His covenant people to recognize and distinguish His holy thing, including the holy anointing oil from all others.

2) **Not To Be Poured Upon Man's Flesh**

The anointing oil was not to be used as an ointment or

cologne for outward adorning. It was meant to be a holy oil for anointing. Thus the Lord specified it should not be put on man's flesh. The psalmist affirmed this when he wrote, **"...thou anointest my head with oil; my cup runneth over..." (Ps 23:5)** The anointing is not for showmanship, but for the ministry.

3) Not To Be Duplicated

The Lord was very particular in warning His people against faking or falsifying the anointing. Ever Ready Batteries advertises batteries with a slogan of, "Get the cat, not a copy cat." In reality, they are saying get the original and not an imitation. The Lord wants the church to operate under the anointing and not under false pretenses or with imitations: not copying what others are doing but rather how He wants to operate. Faking the anointing could invite divine wrath. The anointing of God was upon Paul as he performed signs and wonders in Ephesus. However, when Paul left other people tried to imitate the anointing and failed miserably.

The Scripture declares it this way,

"Then certain of the vagabond Jews, exorcists, took upon them to call over them which had evil spirits the name of the Lord Jesus saying, we adjure you by Jesus whom Paul preacheth. And there were seven sons of one Sceva, a Jew, the chief of priests, which did so. And the evil spirit

answered and said, Jesus I know, and Paul I know, but who are you? And the man in whom the evil spirit was leaped upon them and overcame them, and prevailed against them, so that they fled out of that house naked and wounded" (Acts 1:13-16).

They were faking the anointing. They did not have the real thing. Caution; even the demons could tell the difference between the true anointing and a counterfeit. The Lord does not look upon it kindly when the anointing is falsified or imitated.

4)   Not To Be Poured On A Stranger

This instruction was to protect the value and integrity of the anointing oil. The anointing oil was meant only for those who are in covenant relationship with the God of Israel. In confronting the hypocrisy of the Jews, Jesus said unto them, **"Give not that which is holy unto the dogs, neither cast ye your pearls before a swine, lest they trample them under their feet, and turn again and rend you" (Matthew 7:6).** In other words, the stranger to the covenant relationship, who has no understanding of the anointing and its divine purpose, might defile it and even bring it into disrepute.

When a religious leader falls into a disgrace or any form of moral failure, the anointing is quickly questioned by believers and non-believers alike. To determine if one is under the anointing we must give consideration to the ingredients of the anointing oil and their characteristics. It is important for every believer to realize that the Lord Jesus Christ is our only true standard of the anointing. He is indeed the Christ, the anointed one on whom the Holy Spirit rested **(See Matthew, 3:16&17).**

While seeking the anointing is extremely essential, it is equally essential for the believer to experience a continued overflow of the anointing. I do not believe that the Lord intends for His church to experience a short-lived revival today and walk in weakness and carnality till another revival comes along. Like Elisha, the church of Jesus Christ must seek the anointing for a daily life of spiritual fulfillment and joy in the Holy Ghost. The church must realize that the anointing is not optional if we are to carry on the divine mandate victoriously. This explains why Elisha sought a double portion of the anointing from his master, Elijah, before he was taken away by the Lord **(II Kings 2:9).** How to experience a double portion of the anointing or continued renewal will be discussed in the next chapter.

Chapter 9

Steps To Receiving Fresh Anointing/ Renewal

And it came to pass when they were gone over, that Elijah said to Elisha, ask what I shall do for thee, before I be taken away from thee. And Elisha said, I pray thee, let a double portion of the spirit be upon me. **(II Kings 2:9)**

Elisha had recognized the anointing on his master Elijah. He suddenly became aware that the time had come for Elijah to be taken away by the Lord. In fact, this impending departure of his master Elijah was confirmed by the sons of the prophets in every city they went. Elisha also knew that he would have to carry on the ministry after Elijah was taken away by the Lord **(see I kings 19:16).** Elisha was also aware that the ministry could only be carried out in Elijah's absence with an anointing from God.

He waited on Elijah with expectancy like the disciples did in the upper room **(See Acts 1:4&5).** Elisha was not ready to let Elijah out of his sight until he received a double portion of the anointing that was upon him **(See II Kings, 2:9).** He journeyed with Elijah from Gilgal to the Jordan River with expectancy.

The Scripture describes the journey this way,

"And it came to pass, when the LORD would take up Elijah into heaven by a whirlwind that Elijah went with Elisha from Gilgal. And Elijah said unto Elisha, Tarry here, I pray thee; for the LORD hath sent me to Bethel. And Elisha said unto him, As the LORD liveth, and as thy soul liveth, I will not leave thee. So they went down to Bethel. And the sons of the prophets that were at Bethel came forth to Elisha, and said unto him, Knowest thou that the LORD will take away thy master from thy head today? And he said, Yea, I know it; hold ye your peace. And Elijah said unto him, Elisha, tarry here, I pray thee; for the LORD hath sent me to Jericho. And he said, As the LORD liveth, and as thy soul liveth, I will not leave thee. So they came to Jericho. And the sons of the prophets that were at Jericho came to Elisha, and said unto him,

Knowest thou that the LORD will take away thy master from thy head today? And he answered, Yea, I know it; hold ye your peace. And Elijah said unto him, Tarry, I pray thee, here; for the LORD hath sent me to Jordan. And he said, As the LORD liveth, and as thy soul liveth, I will not leave thee. And they two went on. And fifty men of the sons of the prophets went, and stood to view afar off: and they two stood by Jordan. And Elijah took his mantle, and wrapped it together, and smote the waters, and they were divided hither and thither, so that they two went over on dry ground" (II Kings 2:1-8).

It must be noted that the granting of a double portion of the anointing was not Elijah's to give. This is something that only God can grant. However, we must consider the Old Testament concept of double portion of the inheritance for the firstborn. Elisha, having faithfully served Elijah who had no offspring, was most likely asking to be treated as his firstborn son. In the New Testament church, the disciples were refilled on a couple of occasions as they sought the Lord for power to carry on the divine mandate assigned them.

The disciples prayed for renewal saying,

"And now, Lord, behold their threatenings: and grant unto thy servants, that with all boldness they

may speak thy word, By stretching forth thine hand to heal; and that signs and wonders may be done by the name of thy holy child Jesus. And when they had prayed, the place was shaken where they were assembled together; and they were all filled with the Holy Ghost, and they spake the word of God with boldness"** (Acts 4:29-31).

It is therefore appropriate for a believer, and the church as a whole, to ask for flesh anointing, double portion or renewal to do the work of the Lord.

Jesus alluded to the need and the possibility for flesh anointing or renewal when He told the parable about the old wineskin and the new wine. The scriptures declare,

"**And he spake also a parable unto them; No man putteth a piece of a new garment upon an old; if otherwise, then both the new maketh a rent, and the piece that was taken out of the new agreeth not with the old. And no man putteth new wine into old wineskins; else the new wine will burst the bottles, and be spilled, and the wineskins shall perish. But new wine must be put into new wineskins; and both are preserved**" (Luke **5:36-38**). Proper interpretation of the original Greek text suggests something like this, **"put a new wine in a renewed wineskin"**.

Thus the Lord was telling the Jews to put a new wine in renewed wineskins. The customary process to renew an old wineskin was by placing the old wineskin in olive oil for a period of time. As the wineskin soaked up oil it regained its elasticity and ability to hold not just a new wine, but more wine without breaking up. This indicates that there is a possibility of renewal for the believer with flesh oil to be revived and rejuvenated for the work of the Lord. Elisha's request for a double portion was most possibly a request for flesh anointing or renewal to continue the prophetic ministry after the Lord had taken away his master, Elijah.

Elisha faithfully and patiently followed his master, Elijah from Gilgal to the River Jordan where the Lord took him away. Though not an exhaustive exposition, the historical events at these cities give some significant spiritual insights to the believer on how to experience a renewal or receive a double portion of the anointing. We must keep in mind that the sequence with which this is dealt in this chapter is not necessarily how the sovereign Lord should operate. The Lord is able to anoint his people at His own timing and place He chooses.

Step One: Gilgal (A New Beginning)

From this city of Gilgal the journey began for Elijah and Elisha. This town of Gilgal had been the site of great and significant events in the history of the Jews. This was the first place the Jews encamped upon crossing the Jordan River on dry ground **(See Joshua 4:19-23)**. Their new life in the Promised Land began here. Here at Gilgal, the Lord instructed Joshua to circumcise all the men who were born during the wilderness journey in accordance with His covenant with Abraham **(See Joshua, 5:1-8).** Thus they had renewed their commitment to the covenant by their circumcision. The Lord spoke to Joshua after the circumcision saying, **"…this day have I rolled back the reproach of Egypt from off you. Wherefore the name of the place is called Gilgal unto this day"** **(Joshua 5:9).** Their past had been rolled away and been ushered into a fresh start. The believer seeking renewal or a flesh anointing must be ready to turn away from the past to allow the Lord to have His way with him of her.

Here at Gilgal the children of Israel celebrated the Passover Feast for the first time in the Promised Land. The Scripture says, **"And the children of Israel encamped in Gilgal, and kept the Passover in the fourteenth day of the month in the plains of Jericho" (Joshua 5:10).** They are now in their inheritance - the Promised Land and comfortable enough to celebrate the Passover feast to commemorate their deliverance from Egypt when the firstborn of their slave masters, including their animals died **(See Exodus 12:12-20).**

Also at Gilgal, the manna ceased and the children of Israel, for the first time ate the fruit of the Promised Land **(See Joshua 5:10&11).**

Gilgal affords the believer a spiritual principal of letting go of the past and moving into a new arena of openness in total surrender to the Lord. This is the obedience that allows the Lord to do new things in our lives.

The Lord affirmed the new thing He desires to do for His people saying,

> **"Remember ye not the former things, neither consider the things of old. Behold, I will do a new thing; now it shall spring forth; shall ye not know it? I will even make a way in the wilderness, and rivers in the desert. The beast of the field shall honor me, the dragons and the owls: because I give waters in the wilderness, and rivers in the desert, to give drink to my people, my chosen. This people have I formed for myself; they shall show forth my praise" (Isaiah 43:18 21).**

We all need the Gilgal experience to have a fresh start with total surrender and openness to the Lord. This is exactly what happened to the early disciples when they turned from their old traditions to wait on the Lord for the outpouring of the Holy Spirit **(See Acts, 2:1-4).**

The Gilgal experience will move the believer from religiosity into a deeper relationship with the Lord. This is because the keys to the car of our lives and ministries are turned over unto the Lord for His absolute control. Such a life is destined to experience continual renewal or fresh anointing to do God's will.

Step Two: Bethel (The House of God)

Bethel was the first stop in their journey from Gilgal. The spiritual significance of Bethel could be traced to the experience of Jacob in that city. It was here that Jacob had his first encounter with God. He had a vision of a ladder from the earth to the heavens with angels ascending and descending on it.

It was this experience that made Jacob changed the name of the city from Luz to Bethel, the House of God **(Genesis 28:10-22)**. It was also here that Jacob made a vow to present a tenth of whatever he acquired to The Lord. His experience in The House of God has transformed the sub-planter into a giver.

Upon Jacob's return from his uncle Laban with his new family and all his substance, he went back to Bethel to worship the Lord. This time he asked his family to sanctify themselves and be disposed of all their pagan ornaments before going to Bethel to worship. His experience at this time was so intense and significant that Jacob called the name of the place El Bethel which means the Lord of The House of God **(Genesis, 35:1-16)**.

Being in the House of God or in His presence affords the believer the opportunity to hear and know His perfect will. David expressed his utmost desire to be in the presence of the Lord, when he wrote, **"I was glad when they said unto me, let us go into the house of the Lord" (Psalm 122:1)**. He wrote again, saying, **"Surely goodness and mercy shall follow me all the days of my life; and I will dwell in the house of the Lord forever" (Psalm**

23:6). There is no other way to receive a flesh anointing or be renewed than in His presence. If a believer wants to experience a flesh release of anointing he or she can never be too busy to wait on the Lord. Isaiah clearly stated the blessings of waiting on the Lord this way, **"But they that wait on the Lord shall renew their strength; they shall mount up with wings like eagles; they shall ran and not be weary. And they shall walk and not faint" (Isaiah, 40:31).** The disciples waited in His presence and received an outpouring of the Holy Spirit **(See Luke 24:49; Acts, 2:4&5).** It is so sad to note that the church today has become so programmed that we try to run through a list of items on the church bulletin during worship, rather than waiting patiently on the Lord. As a result, we often go through the emotions with a form of godliness without the power of God.

Upon Jacob's return from his uncle Laban with his new family and all his substance, he went back to Bethel to worship the Lord. This time he asked his family to sanctify themselves and be disposed of all their pagan ornaments before going to Bethel to worship. His experience at this time was so intense and significant that Jacob called the name of the place El Bethel which means the Lord of The House of God **(Genesis, 35:1-16).**

Step Three: Jericho (Focusing on the Lord)

The next stopping place in their journey was Jericho. The significant events that took place in this city both in the Old and the New Testament times point to the importance of focusing undivided attention on the Lord. Joshua's successful expedition in Jericho was the result of the people focusing their attention on the Lord by following the Ark of the Covenant as the Lord had instructed **(Joshua, 6:10-17).** They knew the walls of Jericho were fortified and even appeared insurmountable, yet they focused their attention and faith in the Lord who had promised them the land for their inheritance. Fear could have gripped them if they had focused on the walls or on their limited resources. Looking to the Lord will make even the highest mountains become like ant hills. The song writer put it like this,

> *Turn your eyes upon Jesus,*
> *And look forth into his wonderful face,*
> *And the things on earth will grow strangely deem,*
> *In the light of his glory and grace.*

Looking to the Lord in obedience leads to confidence that makes deliverance and restoration possible. It was in Jericho that Barthameus, though blind, set his faith towards the direction of the Lord with loud cries, **"Jesus son of David have mercy on me." (See Mark 10:48-52).** He got Jesus' attention and was healed.

It was here in Jericho that Zaccheus focused on the Lord from a sycamore tree. He got the Lord's attention. The Lord invited him down, forgave and restored him **(See Luke, 19:1-10).** Physical and spiritual renewals are all possible for the people of God, if only we shall set our affections on the Lord. The Jericho experience requires that the believer does not set his attention on man but on the one who is able to open the windows of heaven and pour the showers of blessings upon the church. The author of the book of Hebrews put it this way, **"Looking unto Jesus the author and finisher of our faith…." (Hebrews, 12:2).**

Step Four: Jordan (Confirmations)

The Jordan River was the last stop before Elijah was taken away. This was a river of some major historical significance in the history of the Jews. It was at the Jordan River that the Lord magnified Joshua with the miraculous crossing of the Jordan as a confirmation of his leadership before all the children of Israel. The Scripture declares it this way, **"And the Lord said unto Joshua: this day will I begin to magnify thee in the sight of all Israel, that they may know that, as I was with Moses, so I will be with thee" (Joshua 3:7; See also Joshua 2:10&11).**

Elijah split the river into two and walked to the other side with Elisha by the stroke of his mantle. Elisha, after picking up the mantle of Elijah, smote the river with it and it opened in two for him to walk back to the other side **(See II Kings, 2)**. It was at this point that the sons of the prophets realized that Elisha had received an anointing like Elijah's. It was at this place that the ministry of Elisha was confirmed in the eyes of the sons of the prophets.

The Messiaship of Jesus was confirmed at His baptism in

the Jordan River to John the Baptist. As Jesus was coming out of the water, the Holy Spirit came to settle on Him with a divine confirmation pronounced from heaven saying, **"...This is my beloved son, in whom I am well pleased" (Matthew 3:17)."**

For the believer to experience a renewal or a flesh anointing, he or she must not rush into action. Performance mentality has made many believers put themselves in the position of working for God, rather than waiting to be confirmed by the Holy Spirit for the Lord to work through them. Performance mentality leads to the absence of joy and burnout in ministry. When the believer is confirmed by the Holy Spirit, he or she is energized with anointing to accomplish God's purpose.

There is a high rate of spiritual decline in the church today. It appears many who have experienced the Holy Spirit baptism are declining in their spiritual walk into the doldrums of compromise and lukewarmness. Many are leading a defeatist life and experiencing no joy of the Lord. The testimony of many has become void of passion and praise to the Lord, and filled with self aggrandizements. The church needs to be renewed by inviting the Lord to take His rightful place as the Head of the Church, the King of kings and the Lord of lords. The journey of Elijah and Elisha from Gilgal through Bethel, Jericho and finally to the Jordan can afford the believer some great spiritual nuggets to enrich his or her devotional life, worship and spiritual pursuit. It is only then that the life of the believer will fulfill these words of Jesus, **"Let**

your light so shine before men, that they may see your good works, and glorify your father which is in heaven" (Matthew 5:17). What a worship to our Lord would it be for the world to see our good works of faith and recognize as Oral Roberts put it that **"God is a good God."**

Now, The Rest Of The Story

The children of Israel saw a great move of God from Egypt into the Promised Land. Suddenly they turned away from their God into apostasy. The book of Judges describes their state of spiritual and moral decay this way, **"In those days there were no kings in Israel; every man did that which was right in his own eyes" (Judges 2:25, also see Judges 17:6, Judges 18:1).** Then was the great revival under Kings David and Solomon. That revival slowly died out, resulting in rebellion, apostasy and a divided kingdom. Both the northern and the southern kingdoms eventually went into captivity in Assyria and Babylon respectively. Then came the revival under Zerubbabel after 70 years in Babylon. Even though the Lord desires his people to stay revived, the history of the Jews and the Church shows that revivals come and are often sadly followed by a period of spiritual decline, complacency and in some cases apostasy. The questions facing us now are these: "Did this revival under Zerubbabel last? Did the children of Israel remain faithful to the Lord? What happened to the Temple worship after Zerubbabel and the elders past away?

For answers to these questions and what the Lord did to bring his people back into fellowship, look out for Volume II of Phases of Revival—*Ezra Leadership: Restoring the Worship.*

About the Author

Born in Ghana, West Africa, K Bobie Amankwatia, lives in Pennsylvania with his wife Tonya and their two sons, Scott and Daniel. K. Bobie has served in various ministry capacities as a Missionary, Bible teacher and church Planter. He pastored for over 14 years with the Church of God in Liberia. Between 1977 and 1990 he was used of the Lord to plant over 10 churches. He also served as the pastor of the Hope Christian Fellowship in Florida for 7 years before relocating to Pennsylvania. He was also the host and Bible teacher on a weekly radio broadcast, **Moments of Hope** in Clearwater, Florida, He is presently the Overseas Missions Representative for the Royal Gate Missions of Ghana, West Africa. He has authored 3 tracts, **The Prisoner, The way that Seemeth Right, and Seven Steps to Peace** which had been used in Prison and Hospital ministries in Liberia West Africa. He currently works in the field of Christian Counseling.

Need additional copies?

To order more copies of
Phases of Revival - Volume 1
Zerubbabel Leadership: *Rebuilding the Temple*
contact NewBookPublishing.com

- ❏ Order online at NewBookPublishing.com
- ❏ Call 877-311-5100 or
- ❏ Email Info@NewBookPublishing.com

Call for multiple copy discounts!